What the (Active Verb) Is Wrong with the Right?

What the (Active Verb) Is Wrong with the Right?

A Fill-in-the-Blanks Game for the Rest of Us

Shelby Gragg and Stefan Petrucha

THE NEW PRESS

NEW YORK
LONDON

Published in the United States by The New Press, New York, 2011
Distributed by Perseus Distribution

LIBRARY OF CONGRESS CATALOGING-IN-PUBLICATION DATA
Gragg, Shelby.
What the (active verb) Is Wrong with the Right? : a fill-in-the-blanks game for the rest of us
Shelby Gragg and Stefan Petrucha.
p.cm.
ISBN 978-1-59558-638-4 (pb)
1. United States--Politics and government--2001-2009--Humor. 2. United States--Politics and government--2009--Humor. 3. Conservatism--United States--Humor. 4. Right and left (Political science)--Humor. 5. Political culture--United States--Humor. 6. Political satire, American. I. Petrucha, Stefan. II. Title.
E902.G725 2011
973.93--dc22
2010047469

The New Press was established in 1990 as a not-for-profit alternative to the large, commercial publishing houses currently dominating the book publishing industry. The New Press operates in the public interest rather than for private gain, and is committed to publishing, in innovative ways, works of educational, cultural, and community value that are often deemed insufficiently profitable.

www.thenewpress.com

Book design and composition by Shelby Gragg
This book was set in Officina Serif

Printed in the United States of America

2 4 6 8 10 9 7 5 3 1

Contents

Selections

You've Heard It Before

You're watching television, reading the paper or the Web, and you run across something that gives your brain a charley horse. You read it again, rewind it over and over, and the thought runs through your head: "Who the hell makes this crap up?" We don't know for sure, but now it's *your* chance! Now you can learn firsthand that it isn't as easy to be completely batshit crazy 24/7 as it seems on TV.

On these pages you will find direct quotes, excerpts, and amalgams culled from some of our brightest lights. Of course, like true high schoolers, we measure "brightest" in terms of popularity, not intelligence. You know the roll call: Palin, Beck, O'Reilly, Hannity, Cheney, and all those amazing fringe groups that know how to organize via the Internet but still can't wrap their heads around the concept of evolution and have somehow earned the media's undivided attention.

And who can forget Christine O'Donnell? No, really. If anyone out there knows a way to forget her, please tell us how.

These passages have had their crazy surgically removed, leaving you the opportunity to let *your* crazy shine through! In the process, you may create a grammatically correct sentence, but can you surpass the genius of the original? On the other hand, you can also play for geek cred — do you know your subject well enough to re-create the original intent?

With any luck, when you are done, you will have a newfound appreciation for the effort that goes into stoking the fires of hatred and ensuring blind, unthinking obedience to invisible masters. Hopefully, in laughing at these inanities, you'll relieve some of your own fear and shock over the fact that these very voices have entranced so many others with their dim-witted siren call.

How It's Done

As with similar games, various parts of speech in these passages have been blanked out. A game pundit is chosen from among the players by either dice roll or combat. The pundit selects a passage, then, cleverly concealing it by holding up the back of the book, asks for the type of word needed for each blank.

The others, perhaps in an ordered manner, call out their creative answers. When the passage is complete, the pundit reads the results. Hilarity and a lowered opinion of the human race ensue.

Sometimes the requested word will be a mere noun or verb, others a jingoistic phrase, arcane religious group, body part, or patriotic symbol. For example, here's an actual quote from a popular right-winger with one phrase missing:

"I have to tell you, I hate Woodrow Wilson *(dead person)* with everything in me. God bless you."

Wasn't that easy? Now, if there is a number next to the word, it's a repeating item, as in the following, which is not a direct quote but appears here for illustrative purposes:

I have to tell you, I hate ________________ *(dead person 1)* with everything in me. I hate ________________ *(dead person 1)* so much, if they weren't dead I'd kill them. God bless you.

Lastly, rather than ask for different word forms, such as a gerund (a term we didn't know until our editor told us about it), or plural or past tense, we simply ask for the basic word type and add the appropriate letters, as in:

I'm sick and tired of all the ________________*s* *(group member)* __________*ing* *(verb)* my __________*s* *(noun)*. I should've __________*ed* *(verb)* them a long time ago! God bless you.

Clever game players may come up with idiomatic answers that don't easily fit our simple constructs. We have full faith in the pundit to fill in the appropriate grammatical form for the enjoyment of all. To get the ball rolling, a suggested word list appears at the back of the book starting on page 113.

FYI - it's Glenn Beck who has the curious dislike of
our 28th President, Woodrow Wilson.

The Constitution & The Bill of Right-Wingers

Listening to the right, you'd think that the Constitution has been rewritten since we studied it in school. Below is a somewhat redacted version. Please fix it, please!

We the _______________s of the United __________s, in order to
(*group member*) (*noun*)
form a more __________ __________, establish ______________, insure
(*adjective*) (*noun*) (*abstraction*)
domestic _______________, provide for the common
(*emotional state*)
______________, promote the general welfare, and secure the blessings
(*demographic*)
of ______________ to ourselves and ____________, do ordain and establish
(*abstraction*) (*celebrity*)
this Constitution.

All rules within shall be binding for all persons and ______________
(*mass medium*)
either in current use or to be discovered in the future, excluding

________________, ____________ and __________________,
(*major corporation*) (*celebrity*) (*followers of religion*)
except in the case of __________________, attack from
(*medical side effect*)
________________, ________________, with the full understanding
(*form of government*) (*pagan religion*)
of the following:

Freedom of __________________ is not freedom from
(*inalienable right 1*)
________________, so we have to do whatever ________________ says.
(*inalienable right 1*) (*religious leader*)

A well regulated __________, being necessary to the security
(*group*)
of a free State, the right of the ________________s to keep
(*group member*)
and bear ____________s including in retail outlets such
(*weapon*)
as ________________, shall not be abridged unless pried from their
(*major chain store*)
cold, dead ______________s.
(*appendage*)

No ________________ shall in time of peace be quartered in any house,
(group member)
without the consent of ___________.
(celebrity)

The right of the people to be secure against unreasonable ___________s
(noun)
and _________s, shall not be violated, unless there is reason to suspect
(noun)
they are a ________________ in which case all bets are off.
(group member)

No person shall be held to answer for a crime except on presentment or indictment of a Grand Jury, unless there is reason to suspect they are a ________________, in which case all bets are off.
(group member)

The accused shall enjoy the right to a speedy and public trial unless there is reason to suspect they are a ________________, in which case all
(group member)
bets are off.

The right of trial by jury shall be preserved, unless there is reason to suspect the accused is a ________________, in which case all bets are off.
(group member)

Excessive bail shall not be required, nor excessive fines imposed, nor cruel and unusual punishments inflicted unless there is reason to suspect the accused is a ________________, in which case all bets are off.
(group member)

The enumeration here of certain rights shall not be construed to deny other rights retained by the people unless there is reason to suspect they are ________________s, in which case all bets are off.
(group member)

Powers not delegated to the United States by the Constitution, nor prohibited by it to the States, are reserved to ____________________,
(famous TV personality)
respectively, or ____________________.
(superhero, Marvel or DC)

A Brief Sanity: The Military Industrial Complex

The 1950's icon of conservatism President Dwight Eisenhower felt it necessary to warn the nation of what he saw as an imminent threat to America. In many ways, this was the last gasp of sanity to issue from the right. It's been a race to the bottom ever since. Below is a truncated version of his famous speech.

A vital element in keeping the __________ *(noun)* is our military. Our ______________ *(appendages)* must be mighty, ready for instant__________ing *(verb)*, so no potential aggressor may be tempted to risk his own __________________ *(type of collection)*. Yet our military organization today bears little relation to that known by the fighting ______________________ *(species, real or mythic)* of World War II or Korea. The U.S. had no armaments industry. American makers of ________________s *(good or service)* could make swords as well.

Now we have been compelled to create a permanent _________________s *(good or service)* industry of _________ *(size)* proportions. The total influence — economic, political, even _______________________ *(adjective ending in -al)* — is felt in every city, every Statehouse, every _______________ *(type of room)* of the Federal government. Our toil, resources, and __________s *(noun)* are all involved; so is the very structure of _______________________ *(favorite 1950s TV show)*.

Largely responsible for the changes has been the ____________________ *(adjective ending in -al)* revolution during recent ________________ *(period of time)*. ______________________ *(type of entertainment)* has become central; it also becomes more formalized, complex, and costly. Today, the solitary _______________ *(famous geek)* tinkering in his _______________ *(type of room)* has been overshadowed by __________________s *(group member)* in _________ *(place)*.

The ______________________ university, historically the ____________
(large amount of money) (body part)
of ________________-ideas and discovery, has experienced a
(amount of money)
revolution in the conduct of ________________. Partly because of
(a leisure activity)
the huge _____________s involved, a government contract becomes a
(appendage)
substitute for ___________ _________.
(adjective) (noun)

We must now ________ against unwarranted influence by
(verb)
the ____________________ industrial complex. We must never
(popular game console)
let the weight of this combination endanger our ______________
(favorite food)
or ________________. We should never take _________________
(biological process) (amount of money)
for granted. Only an alert and knowledgeable __________ can
(animal)
compel the proper meshing of the huge industrial machinery with

our _____________________ and ____________________.
(home studio component) (type of cable adapter)

It is the task of statesmanship to mold, to balance, and to ________
(verb)
these and other ________________ within the principles of
(electronic devices)
our democratic system — ever aiming toward the supreme goals of

free _______________s.
(consumer good)

A Good Republican Coating

Even Eisenhower's vice president managed to come across as reasonable when he felt called upon to defend his ethics. Yeah, we know, hindsight and all . . . but here's a brief look at Nixon's famous "Checkers" speech.

My fellow ______________________s, I come before you as
(nationality, real or mythic)
a ______________ whose integrity has been questioned. I'm sure
(group member)
you've heard I took ____________________ from __________.
(outrageous sum of money) *(group)*
It was not just illegal, it was wrong, but only if any of it went
to my ________________. Now let me say this about that:
(personal luxury 1)
Every _____________ was used to pay for that _______________.
(foreign coin) *(personal luxury 1)*

A Senator gets _________________ a year, enough to pay for one
(large sum of money)
trip to ______________. He also gets an allowance for _________.
(vacation spot) *(vice)*
But then, you say, "Well, how do you pay for your _________?" The
(vice)
first way is to be a _________________. I don't happen to be
(illegal profession 1)
a _________________ so I couldn't use that one. The only way was to
(illegal profession 1)
accept ___________s. I am proud of the fact that not one of them has
(animal)
ever asked me for ________.
(food)

Some of you may say, "Well, that's all right, but have you got
any ____________?" Just an hour ago we received an audit which I have
(illegal drug)
in my ____________ which concludes that I do not. Now that, my friends,
(body part)
is not Nixon speaking, but ______________. Some will say: Maybe you
(famous puppet)
were able to fake this thing. How can we believe what you say?

Pat and I have the satisfaction that every _______________ we've got
(foreign coin)
is ___________ ours. Pat doesn't have a(n) ____________________ coat.
(adverb) (endangered species)
But she does have a respectable Republican ____________________ coat.
(endangered species)
I always tell her she'd look good in ____________________.
(endangered species)

We did get one gift — after the election, a little ___________ sent all
(animal)
the way from ____________________. Black and white spotted. And our little
(fictional location)
girl Tricia named it _________________. And I just want to say this right
(mobster name)
now, that regardless of what they say about it, we're gonna _________ it.
(verb)

And just let me say this. We hear a lot about _____________ these days
(fast food)
but I say, why can't we have prosperity built on ______________ rather
(snack food)
than on war?

Finally, I know you wonder whether or not I am going to stay on the
Republican __________. I don't believe that I ought to _________ because
(noun) (verb)
I'm not a(n) ____________________. And, incidentally, Pat's not
(illegal profession 2)
a(n) ____________________ and neither is ____________. I'm going
(illegal profession 2) (mobster)
to continue this fight until we _________ ____________________ and
(verb) (1950's rock group)
the ____________________ and those that defend them out of
(political fringe group)
Washington. Thank you and good ____________________.
(non-Christian holiday)

I Have a List . . . Really, I Do!

As it turned out, we didn't have long to wait for the outrageous distortions of the right to begin. A little-known senator from Wisconsin, Joseph McCarthy, revealed to the nation he had a list of 207, or 57, or 81, or . . . nevermind, he didn't have any names. But after that he did have the nation's attention. How'd that work out?

McCarthy: Mr. Welch has in his law firm ________________, *(stripper name 1)* who has been a member of an organization which has done more to defend ____________ *(group 1)* and the ____________ *(group 1)* cause than anyone. I am not asking why you tried to _________ *(verb)* him, whether you knew he was a ____________________ *(member of group 1)* or not, I don't know. I don't think you would ever knowingly aid the ____________ *(group 1)*, but I think you are unknowingly__________ing *(verb)* it just the same.

Welch: Senator McCarthy, I think until this moment, I think I never really gauged your _________ *(vice)* or your __________________ *(piece of clothing)*. __________________ *(stripper name 1)* is a young ___________ *(gender)* who went to ________________ *(famous school)* and is starting what looks to be a brilliant career with us. I fear s/he shall always bear a ________________ *(type of wound)* needlessly inflicted by you. If it were in my power to _______________ *(negative verb)* you for your ____________________ *(negative adjective)* cruelty, I will do so. I like to think I am a(n) ______________ *(occupation)*, but your forgiveness will have to come from _____________ *(celebrity)*.

McCarthy: Mr. Welch talks about this being cruel and ________________. I just give this man's record.
(negative adjective)
In ________ ________________ was . . .
(year) *(stripper name 1)*

Welch: May we not ______________ this? You have done enough.
(negative verb)
Have you no sense of ________________ sir, at long last? Have you left
(one of five senses)
no sense of ________________?
(one of five senses)

McCarthy: I know this ______________s you, Mr. Welch. But I may
(negative verb)
say, on a point of personal ________ and I would like to ______________
(vice) *(negative verb)*
it — unless we make sure that there is no__________ing of our Government
(verb)
by _________, then just as certain as you ______________ there, in the
(group) *(negative verb)*
period of our lives you will see a(n) ________ world. There is no question
(color)
about that.

Ronnie-Care

In 1961, as part of the American Medical Association's "Operation Coffee Cup," actor Ronald Reagan put out a record album *(remember those?)* to help lobby against the creation of Medicare. We all need to be grateful for his powers of persuasion. Can you do better?

It's very easy to ________ *(verb)* a medical program as a ____________ *(adjective)* project, most people are a little ____________ *(adjective)* to oppose anything that suggests ______________________ *(adjective ending in -al)* care for people who possibly can't afford it.

The American people, if you put it to them about ____________________ *(undesirable adjective 1)* medicine, would unhesitatingly vote against it. Under the ____________ *(president)* administration, it was proposed that we have a(n) ____________________ *(undesirable adjective 1)* health insurance program for all people in the United States, and, of course, the American people __________ *(adverb)* rejected this.

Now in our country under our ________________ *(economic system)* system we have seen medicine reach ____________________ *(comparative adjective)* heights than it has in any country in the world. Today, the __________ *(noun)* between patient and doctor in this country is something to be ____________ *(adjective)* about. The privacy, the care that is given to a person, the right to chose a(n) ___________ *(noun 1)*, the right to go from one ___________ *(noun 1)* to the other.

This is a(n) ____________ *(U.S. icon)* that I wonder if any of us has a right to take from any __________ *(species)*. All of us can see what happens once you establish the precedent that the _________________ *(collective noun 1)* can determine a man's

working place and his working methods, determine his _________.
(noun)
From here it's a short step to all the rest of __________________, to
(political system 1)
determining his pay.

Pretty soon your son won't decide when he's in school, where he will go, or what he will do for a living. He will wait for the ___________________to
(collective noun 1)
tell him where he will go to _________ and what he will do.
(verb)

We talk ___________________ today, and strangely, we let
(political system 2)
___________________ begin to assume the aspect of ___________________,
(political system 2) *(electoral method)*
is all that is needed. The "_________________" is a fine aspect
(electoral method)
of ___________________ provided there are guarantees written into our
(political system 2)
government concerning the rights of the individual and of the minorities.

At the moment, the key issue is, we do not want to __________________
(undesirable verb)
medicine.

We Don't Need No Education

During the civil rights era, the vitriol continued to increase. Alabama governor George Wallace's June 11, 1963, speech on the schoolhouse steps may have been the last big chance for Americans to openly display their prejudice. And yes, he was a Democrat.

I do not stand here in ________________ for defiance sake.
(type of clothing)
I do not stand here simply to block these two ________________s
(group member)
from entering this ________________. In a sense, I just happen to be
(retail location)
standing here. They are fine ________________s and under other
(group member)
circumstances I'd be delighted to ________ them in my own home.
(verb)
My action seeks to avoid having state sovereignty sacrificed on the altar
of ______________. The __________-induced intrusion upon the campus
(pagan god) *(drug)*
of the University of Alabama today offers a ________________ example
(negative adjective)
of the oppression of the sovereignty of this State.

While ________________ may applaud these acts, ______________
(huge number) *(tiny number)*
Americans will gaze in ________________ upon this attempt to
(emotional state)
subordinate the rights of Alabama. This nation was never meant to be a
unit of ________________, but a united ___________ of the many.
(small number) *(weapon)*
This is the reason our ______________________-loving forefathers
(addictive drug or food)
established ______________, ensuring that no ________________ could
(retail outlet) *(group member)*
gain ________________s.
(powerful object)

We are a ____________ *(something scary)*-fearing people — not a ____________ *(something not so scary)* -fearing people, though I freely admit that ____________ *(something icky)* gives me the willies. We practice today the free heritage bequeathed to us by the founding ________s *(relative)*.

Further, as the ____________ *(leadership title)* of Alabama, it is my duty to see that the ________s *(noun)* are executed. I stand before you in place of ____________ *(tiny number)* other ____________s *(group member)* whose presence would have confronted you had they not been busy ________ing *(verb)*. It is the right of every citizen to ________ *(verb)* courageously against ____________ *(civil right)* regardless of the truth.

Therefore, I George C. Wallace do hereby denounce and ________ *(verb)* this ____________ *(derogatory adjective)* and ____________ *(derogatory adjective)* action by ________ *(group)*. Segregation at ____________ *(time of day)*, segregation on ________ *(holiday)*, and segregation for ____________ *(period of time)*.

Not that I am prejudiced or anything.

Worn Bill and Loose Change

Bill O'Reilly has become the elder statesman of the right, not only because of his longevity, but also because he now seems reasonable and measured when compared to more recent additions to the roster of the far right. But let's give Bill his due. He can still bring the crazy when he wants. Here are some gems, based on quotes from his show and media appearances. Can you bring it like Bill?

"I couldn't get over the fact that there was no difference between Sylvia's restaurant and any other restaurant. I mean, it was exactly the same, and even though it's run by ____________________*s* *(ethnic group member 1)* and has primarily ____________________*s* *(ethnic group member 1)* patronship. There wasn't one person in Sylvia's who was screaming, '__________ *(obscenity)*, I want more __________ *(beverage)*.' I mean, everybody was — it was like going into a(n) __________ *(ethnicity)* restaurant in an all-__________ *(race)* __________ *(boring location)* in the sense of people were sitting there, and they were __________*ing* *(verb)* and having fun. And there wasn't any kind of ______________________________ *(violent form of political demonstration)* at all."

"I think ____________________*s* *(ethnic group member 1)* are starting to think more and more for themselves. They're getting away from the __________ *(famous person)* and the __________ *(fictional person)*. They're just trying to figure it out. 'Look, I can make it. If I __________ *(virtuous verb)* and get __________ *(adjective)*, I can make it.'"

"That's my advice to all ____________________*s* *(hated group member)*, whether they're in the ____________________ *(virtuous organization)* or in the ____________________ *(patriotic organization)* or in high school: Shut up, don't tell anybody what you do, your life will be a lot ____________________ *(comparative adjective)*."

"I've been in combat. I've ____________ed it, I've been ____________ to it...
(verb) (adjective)

and if my ________________ is in danger, and I've got a(n) ____________,
(secreting organ) (noun 1)

and the ____________ knows where the enemy is, and I'm looking him in
(noun 1)

the eye, the ____________ better tell me. That's all
(noun 1)

I'm gonna tell you. If it's life or death, ____________ is going first."
(noun 1)

"And guys, if you ____________ a girl, it will come back to get you. That's
(verb)

called ________________." — *The O'Reilly Factor for Kids*
(foreign phrase)

"You know what's really ____________? You actually have
(adjective)

a(n) ________________ on this ________________al election. That
(type of criminal) (elected position)

is scary, but it's true. You've got ____________ ____________s watching
(adjective) (noun)

your ____________ show every night and they can vote."
(adjective)

Morals Clause? I Don't Need No Stinkin' Morals Clause!

In 2004 Bill O'Reilly was sued by one of his producers over accusations of sexual harassment. Bill and Fox News settled the suit, so we don't have all the details, but the court filings, quoted in part here, have examples of the high morals he requires of the rest of the world. Can you reach his lofty heights? Go ahead and try.

On or about May 2003, Defendant Bill O'Reilly took Plaintiff and her friend to dinner. During the course of the dinner, O'Reilly repeatedly ____________*ed* (*verb*) the women, singing the praises of ____________ (*sexual activity*), offering to ____________ (*form of communication*) them both, and suggesting that the three of them "go to ____________ (*place*) together and ____________ (*idiom referring to sex 1*)." O'Reilly further suggested that the women needed to be ____________*ed* (*verb*) so they'd be equipped and ready to go when a(n) "____________ (*large animal*) shows up in your lives," and offers to "____________ (*idiom referring to sex 1*)." O'Reilly further suggested they use their sexuality to their advantage so they'd have ____________ (*abstract noun 1*) over men, otherwise men would have ____________ (*abstract noun 1*) over them. Plaintiff was extremely ____________ (*emotional state*) and protested: "Bill, you're my ____________ (*occupation 1*)!"

During the course of this dinner, in approximately May 2003, Defendant Bill O'Reilly, without solicitation or invite, ____________*ed* (*verb*) Plaintiff and her friend with stories concerning his ____________ (*sexual activity*) with a girl in a car at ____________________ *(national monument)*, as well as two "____________________ *(salacious adjective 1)*" ______________ *(nationality 1)* airline stewardesses and a "girl" at a sex show in ___________ *(country)* who'd shown him things in a ______________ *(small vehicle)* that "______________ed *(cathartic verb)* him." Defendant then stated he was going to ___________ *(country)* to meet ______________________ *(ancient religious figure)*, that his pregnant wife was staying at home with his daughter, and implied he was looking forward to some ____________________________ *(commandment-breaking activity)* with the "____________________ *(salacious adjective 1)*" ______________ *(nationality 1)* women. Both Plaintiff and her friend were _________________ *(emotional state)*, but felt powerless to ________ *(verb)* strongly since Defendant was Plaintiff's ______________ *(occupation 1)* and a powerful ___________ *(animal)* at Fox.

Later in the filing, Bill acts up again:

If any woman ever ___________s *(verb)* me, I'll make her pay so dearly that she'll wish she'd never _________________ed *(bodily function)*. I'll rake her through the ___________s *(noun)*, bring up things in her life and make her so _________________ *(emotional state)* that she'll be destroyed. And besides, she wouldn't be able to afford the same ______________________ *(latest device from Apple)* I can, or endure it financially as long as I can. And nobody would believe her, it'd be ____________________ *(derogatory adjective)* and who are they going to believe? Me or some ______________ *(adjective 1)* woman making ______________ *(adjective 1)* accusations. They'd see her as some _____________________ *(derogatory adjective)* ___________ *(noun)*, someone unstable.

I'd never make the mistake of picking unstable ____________ *(derogatory adjective)* girls like that.

During the course of this conversation, Defendant Bill O'Reilly sternly warned, to the effect:

If you cross Fox News Channel, it's not just me, it's ____________ *(TV character 1)* who will go after you. I'm the street guy out front making loud noises about the issues, but ____________ *(TV character 1)* operates behind the scenes, ________*ing* *(verb)* and making things happen so that one day, ____________ *(exclamation)*! The person ________*ed* *(verb)* but never saw it coming. Look at Al Franken, one day he's going to get a ____________ *(display of affection)* and life as he knows it will change forever. That day will happen, trust me.

Gee, he was right! Al Franken's life has changed forever, now he's a U.S. senator. But they probably just called him on the phone.

To give Bill the benefit of the doubt, he may have been reading from his first novel *Those Who Trespass: A Novel of Television and Murder,* which contains the following gems:

"Off with those ____________________s." *(article of clothing)*

"I would like you to unhook your ____________________ *(article of clothing)*, and let it slide down your arm."

"Cup your hands under your ______________s *(body part)* and hold them for ten seconds."

"Say baby, put down that pipe, and get my ____________________ *(plumber's material)* up!"

"She obediently performed ____________________ *(sex act or Shakespeare play)* on him. Five feet away, the other teenage ___________ *(animal)* sat on a __________ *(noun)* on the floor and watched, greedily sucking on a ____________ *(medicine)* pipe Robo had passed to her. Edgar looked over and __________ed *(verb)*, showing yellowed decaying ______________s *(body part)*. Obviously, he preferred oral sex to oral hygiene."

And, "________________ *(exclamation)*, I wish I was ____________________ *(sexual preference)*!"

For the equally delightful original, we highly recommend the audio book, read by the author. It's pure win!

Hail the Conquering Hero

On September 14, 2003, Vice President Cheney appeared on *Meet the Press* with Tim Russert to posit an alternate universe. Was he successful? Not so much. Can you help him make his case?

Russert: If your analysis is not correct, and we're not treated as liberators, but as conquerors, and the Iraqis begin to resist, do you think the American people are prepared for a long, costly, and bloody battle with significant American casualties?

Cheney: Well, I don't think it's likely to __________ *(verb)* that way, Tim, because I really do believe that we will be greeted as ____________s *(noun)*. I've talked with a lot of _________________s *(nationality)* in the last several months myself, had them to the __________________ *(U.S. landmark)*. The read we get on the people of ___________ *(nation)* is that there is no question that they want to the get rid of _____________________ *(well-known person)* and they will welcome as liberators _____________ *(country 1)* when we come to do that.

Russert: The army's top general said that we would have to have several hundred thousand troops there for several years in order to maintain stability.

Cheney: I _________ *(verb)*. We need, obviously, a large ____________ *(noun 1)* and we've deployed a large ___________ *(noun 1)*. To _________ *(verb)*, from a(n) _____________ *(adjective)* standpoint, to achieve our __________ *(noun)*, we will need a(n) _____________ *(adjective)* presence there until such time as we can turn things

over to the ____________________s___ themselves. But to suggest that
(*nationality member*)
we need ________________ troops there after military operations cease,
(*large number*)
after the ______________ ends, I don't think is accurate. I think that's an
(*cultural era*)
overstatement.

Russert: Every analysis said this war itself would cost about $80 billion, recovery of Baghdad, perhaps of Iraq, about $10 billion per year. We should expect as American citizens that this would cost at least $100 billion for a two-year involvement.

Cheney: There are estimates out there. In _____________ you've
(*country 1*)
got a __________ that's got the second-largest __________________
(*noun*) (*consumer good 1*)
reserves in the world, second only to _____________________. It will
(*imaginary country*)
generate ________________ of ____________ a year in cash flow if
(*large number*) (*currency*)
they get back to their production of roughly ____________ barrels
(*number*)
of ___________________ a day.
(*consumer good 1*)

I Never Said What You Made Me Say

Three years later, on September 9, 2006, Vice President Cheney once again stopped by *Meet the Press* with Tim Russert to explain how he was set up, and everything we knew was wrong. Please set him straight.

Russert: ______________ *(public office)*, the primary rationale given for the war in Iraq was ____________ *(person 1)* had ________________*s* *(forbidden object 1)*. You told the ______________ *(organization)*, "Simply stated, there is no doubt that ___________ *(person 1)* now has ________________*s* *(forbidden object 1)*." Based on what you know now, that ____________ *(person 1)* did not possess ________________*s* *(forbidden object 1)* that were described, would you still have gone into __________ *(nation)*?

Cheney: Yes, because — clearly the intelligence that said he did was ____________ *(adjective)*. That was the intelligence all of us saw, that was the intelligence all of us believed, it was — when ____________ *(person 2)* sat in the Oval Office and the president asked him directly, he said, "____________ *(person 2)*, how good is the case against ____________ *(person 1)* on ________________*s* *(forbidden object 1)*?" he said, "It's a ______________ *(sports term)*, Mr. President."

Russert: Leading up to the war, you were on this program and I asked you about an analysis of what could occur. Wasn't your judgment overly rosy? "Greeted as ______________ *(adjective 1)*."

Cheney: You gave me a choice, Tim, "Will you be greeted as ______________ *(adjective 1)* or ______________ *(adjective 2)*?" and I said we'll be greeted as ______________ *(adjective 1)*. And we were.

Russert: But I said what about a long, costly, bloody battle, and you said it's unlikely to unfold that way.

Cheney: And that's true of the battle against the ____________ regime
(person 1)
and his forces. That went very ____________. It was over in a ____________
(adverb) (qualifier)
short period of time. What obviously has developed after that,

the __________, has been long and ____________ and ____________, no
(noun) (adjective) (adjective)
question.

And there was also a personal question that we all wanted to ask.

Russert: Have you been ____________*ing* since February 11, 2006?
(verb 1)

Cheney: No, sir, that was the end of ______________________________
(Warner Bros. cartoon character 1)
season. I have not ____________*ed* since then. But I ordinarily wouldn't
(verb 1)
anyway.

Russert: Have you gotten over that incident?

Cheney: Well, yeah, I don't know that you ever get over it.

Fortunately, ______________________________ is doing very well, he's
(Warner Bros. cartoon character 1)
a good ______________________________ and he could not have been
(Warner Bros. Cartoon character 1)
more gracious or more generous. But it's not the kind of thing I don't think

anybody could ever forget. I certainly won't.

Russert: Should I be relieved you didn't bring your ____________ in
(weapon)
today?

Cheney: I wouldn't worry about it. You're not in season.

Russert: Mr. Vice President, I hope I never am.

Cheney: All right.

You Like Me! You Really Like Me!

In 2008 Arizona senator and presidential aspirant John McCain single-handedly gave us the brightest new star in our political firmament, Sarah Palin. We haven't been able to shake her yet. Here's her debut from the September 3 Republican National Convention.

I accept the call to help our nominee for ______________ *(elective office)* to serve and defend ____________ *(nation 1)*. And I accept the ______________ *(abstract noun 1)* of a tough fight in this election against ______________ *(sinful adjective)* opponents at a(n) ______________ *(emotional state)* hour for our country. And I accept the privilege of ________*ing* *(verb)* with a man who has come through much harder ______________*s* *(abstract noun 1)*, and met far graver challenges, and knows how tough __________*s* *(contest)* are won, the next ______________ *(religious title)* of ____________ *(nation 1)*, ______________ *(famous person)*.

To the families of ____________ *(adjective)* children all across this country, I have a __________ *(noun)* for you: For ____________ *(time span)*, you've sought to make ____________ *(nation 1)* a more ____________ *(adjective)* place for your sons and daughters. And I pledge to you that, if we're elected, you will have a __________ *(noun)* and a __________ *(noun)* in the ______________ *(famous landmark)*.

I had the privilege of ________*ing* *(verb)* most of my life in ______________ *(fast food place)*. I was just your average __________ *(sport 1)* mom and signed up for the ________________ *(fictional organization 1)*. I love those __________ *(sport 1)* moms. You know, they say the difference between a __________ *(sport 1)* mom and the __________ *(cryptid)*? ______________*s* *(nonhuman body part)*.

So I signed up for the ______________ (*fictional organization 1*) because I wanted to make my ________s (*noun*) in public education even better. And when I ran for ______________ (*type of dictator 1*), I didn't need focus groups and voter profiles because I knew those voters, and I knew their ________s (*noun*), too.

I came to office promising major __________ (*virtue 1*) reform to end the culture of __________ (*minority*). And today, that __________ (*virtue 1*) reform is a law. While I was at it, I got rid of a few things in the ______________'s (*type of dictator 1*) office that I didn't believe our ______________ (*demographic*) should have to pay for. That luxury __________ (*vehicle*) was over the top. I put it on ______________ (*famous sale-based Web site*).

Our state's ______________ (*abstract noun*) is under control. We have a __________ (*noun*). And I have protected the ______________ (*demographic*) by __________ing (*verb 1*) wasteful ______________s (*type of produce*), nearly ______________ (*large number*) in ______________s (*type of produce*). We suspended the state fuel tax and ________ed (*verb*) reform to end the ________s (*adjective*) of earmark spending by ______________ (*government institution 1*). I told the ______________ (*government institution 1*), "Thanks, but no thanks," on that Bridge to Nowhere. If our state wanted to build a bridge, we were going to ________ (*verb*) it ourselves.

Thank you, and ________ (*deity*) ________ (*verb*) ________ (*nation*). Thank you.

I'll Be Back

After gaining fame in the 2008 election, then-Governor Palin realized she was destined for greater things. Before she could step onto the big stage, she needed to ditch the locals, which she promptly did, resigning from her post on September 3, 2009.

Hi ____________ *(geopolitical division 1)*, I ____________*al* *(emotional state)* ____________ *(verb)* speaking ____________ *(adverb)* to you, the people I ____________ *(verb)*, as your ____________ *(elective office)*. People who know me know that besides ____________*s* *(noun)* and ____________*s* *(noun)*, nothing's more important to me than our ____________ *(adjective)* ____________ *(geopolitical division 1)*.

So to ____________ *(verb)* the state is a(n) ____________ *(adjective)* ____________ *(noun)*, because I know in my ____________ *(body part)* that ____________ *(geopolitical division 1)* is of such ____________ *(adjective)* importance for ____________ *(geopolitical division 1)*'s ____________ *(noun)*, in our very ____________ *(adjective)* world. And you know me by now, I promised even four years ago to show my ____________ *(body part)* . . . no more conventional "____________ *(hackneyed phrase)*."

The ____________ *(hated group)* ____________*ed* *(adjective)* on ____________ *(geopolitical division 1)*, digging for ____________ *(noun)*. The ethics law I ____________*ed* *(verb)* became their weapon of choice. I've been accused of all sorts of ____________ *(adjective)* ethics violations — such as holding a ____________ *(weapon)* in a photograph, and answering reporters' questions.

If I have ____________*ed* *(verb)* one thing: life is about ____________*s* *(noun)*! ____________*ing* *(verb)* people determine where to put their efforts, choosing to wisely utilize precious ____________ *(noun)*.

I'll work for and campaign for those __________s (*noun*) to be ____________ed (*verb*), as well as those who are ____________ed (*verb*) by our ____________________ (*civil service group*). But I won't do it from the governor's ____________________ (*piece of furniture*). I will not seek reelection as _________________ (*religious title*).

It's not what is best for __________________________ (*geopolitical division 1*). I am ______________ (*adjective*) to take the right path for __________________________ (*geopolitical division 1*) even though it is unconventional and not so comfortable; and I am willing to do so, so that this administration — with its ______________ (*adjective*) agenda, its accomplishments, and its successful ___________ (*noun*) to a(n) ______________ (*adjective*) future — can continue without interruption and with great administrative and legislative ___________________ (*abstract noun*).

Let me go back to a ______________ (*adjective*) analogy for me — sports . . . ____________ (*a sport*). I use it because you're naive if you don't see the national ________________ (*sports term*) drifting away right now. A good ________________ (*sport position*) drives through, protecting the _____________________ (*sports equipment 1*), keeping her ______________ (*body part*) on the ______________________ (*sports equipment 1*) . . . and she knows exactly when to pass the __________________________ (*geopolitical division 1*) so that the team can WIN.

I love my job and I love _________________________ (*geopolitical division 1*). It hurts to make this choice but I am doing what's best for __________________________ (*geopolitical division 1*).

Humble Beginnings: A Tea Party Rally

Not an actual speech, per se, but an amalgam full of familiar phrases. Enjoy! Or . . . tremble!

Who here is a Republican? A Democrat?

A ____________________ *(person with a mental illness)*? It doesn't matter. Here's the real question: Who wants a limited government, free markets, and a(n) ____________ *(appliance)*? Congratulations — you are a part of the Tea Party movement!

More than __________ *(number)* rallies are going on every ______________ *(period of time)*. We are not ______________ *(derogatory term)*. We have been watching and have figured out who needs to go. We are tired of an overbearing __________ *(monster)* trampling the ____________s *(cute animal 1)*. We are real _________s *(noun)*, a real movement. We will cling to our __________s *(weapon)* and ___________s *(appliance)* and let you keep the change.

Why did the founding fathers think speech needed to be ______________ *(dollar amount)* except in the case of ________________ *(major corporation)*? Jesus said: "Ye shall know the truth, and the truth shall make ye ________________ *(psychological disorder)*." This freedom is a right — not a good like ____________ *(illegal trade)*. Every human is born with it, like a ___________ *(body part)*, yet almost every __________ *(monster)* throughout history has tried to ________ *(verb)* it. The Obama administration is doing everything they can to eliminate any ____________s *(cute animal 1)* who disagree with them. They know they can't get their socialist programs passed if right-thinking __________s *(noun)* know the truth, so they try to find a way to pass ____________________s (type of roughage) that eliminate free speech, or resort to calling us _______________ (a bad name) to discredit us.

Now they want to control _________________ (abstract noun) with things like the "________________________ (positive emotional state) doctrine" requiring ________________s (occupation) to present both sides of controversial issues, such as abortion or illegal immigration. Do we want a _______________ (elected post) determining what's fair and balanced? No! A(n) _________________ (unelected post) should do that.

________________s (racist term) will tell you we are racist. ____________________s (homophobic term) will tell you we are homophobes. They'll even say we're ______________________ (derogatory term 3X) and violent. They'll spread lies when in fact they are ______________________ (derogatory term 3X) and deserve ______________________ (violent punishment).

But let me ask you: are we ______________________ (derogatory term 3X)? I know you are, but what am I? Or are we defenders of _________________s (cute animal 1) who will continue to use our First Amendment rights to peacefully assemble ______________________ (dangerous devices) until we get those ______________ (appliances).

Humble Beginings: Birther FAQ or Fiqtion?

He's just not one of us! Not that we're prejudiced or anything! Long before Newt Gingrich classified President Obama's worldview as "Kenyan anticolonial" the birthers have been trying to prove he is foreign born. Here's an amalgam of their thoughts in FAQ form, cobbled from sundry sources.

Why don't you believe Obama was born in Hawaii?

Officials craftily do not say he has a ______________ *(natural act)* certificate, just that his original certificate is in ______________ *(secret place)*. And such a certificate can be issued to a ________________ *(group member)* born anywhere. The original birth certificate may very well be __________________ *(foreign nationality)*. His sister ________________ *(pagan goddess)*, born in Indonesia, also possesses such a certificate, as does __________________ *(fictional character)*.

Since he was on the ballot doesn't that mean he was checked out?

No! In fact a ________________ *(group member)* was on the ballot and received ___________ *(number)* votes.

Haven't the courts dismissed these cases?

Yes, but so what? All we are asking is to let __________________ *(cartoon character)* decide.

What can be done now that he is in office?

Just because a president is in office does not mean he cannot be removed.

The name ________________________ comes to mind. Congress can
(famous movie monster)
impeach him for "High Crimes and ______________*s*." The courts can
(petty crime)
invalidate the election and have him removed from the White House

by ________________________, who can take him to __________.
(children's organization) *(planet)*

If Obama is removed won't ________________*s* riot?
(ethnic group)

They have rioted before. The real threat to America is a possible civil war

if he remains without clearly demonstrating he is a ______________ fan.
(sports team)

If you assume he was born in Hawaii doesn't that make him a natural-born citizen?

If you assume, you make a(n) _____________ of both you and me.
(body part)
What if we assume Osama bin Laden was brought to America for trial and

on one of his ___________'s visits, she becomes pregnant and gives birth
(relative)
to a ___________________? Would that ____________________ be a
(type of monster 1) *(type of monster 1)*
U.S. citizen?

If Obama is proven "a natural-born citizen" will you stop attacking him?

If so, we will unconditionally support his right to be

called ____________________ despite his _____________________ policies
(title for a dictator) *(type of dictatorship)*
that will leave our nation a burnt cinder.

Apologies Are for Wimps

As Americans, we don't expect to apologize for anything. Sometimes, though, it's forced upon us. Here are a few "sorry" examples.

"I have behaved __________ sometimes. Yes, it is true that I was
(adverb)
on ____________________ movie sets and I have done things that
(perjorative adjective)
were not right which I thought then was ______________ but
(positive noun)
now I know that I have ____________ed people. And to those
(verb 1)
people that I have __________ed, I want to say to them I
(verb 1)
am __________ ______________ about that and I apologize because
(adverb) (emotional state)
this is not what I am trying to do."

Arnold Schwarzenegger, candidate for California governor, apologizing for alleged sexual harassment charges from the past thirty years.
– Grade: A- (pretty good)

"I do not consider ____________ evil, and I ________ that
(ethic group) (verb)
my __________ remark may have __________ created that impression."
(adjective) (adverb)

Sen. John McCain (R-AZ) apologizing for referring to Jerry Falwell and Pat Robertson as "forces of evil."
– Grade B (to the point, but he repeats the insult)

"I apologize, but I don't think I had the ______________ vote
(demographic)
anyway."

Louie Welch, candidate for mayor of Houston, apologizing for saying that as part of his four-point plan to prevent the spread of AIDS "one of them is to shoot the queers."
– Grade: C (for effort)

"If I offended ____________ Americans, I regret my choice of words."
(ethnicity)

Rep. John Cooksey (R-LA) apologizing for remarks about people with "a diaper on [their] head."
– Grade: C- (If?)

"We're sorry if this joke, which got a lot of laughs, ________ed anyone."
(verb)

Campaign mgr. for Sen. Jim Bunning (R-KY) apologizing for his boss's saying his opponent resembles one of Saddam Hussein's sons — before his death.
– Grade D (Bunning doesn't even make his own nonapology)

"I wouldn't have said what I said if I'd known the _________ (noun) was on. I would not have taken _________ (deity)'s name in vain, and I _________ (verb) for that because I was not ____________ (adjective), and I am ____________ (adjective) I said something that was not __________ (adverb) ____________ (adjective). So I'd like to _________ (verb) for having said that. But please understand: You're looking at a _________ (noun), and the ______________ (bodily fluid) gets flowing. But I didn't know I was being taped either or I wouldn't have done that."

VP George H.W. Bush apologizing for being caught on mic after a Dan Rather interview saying, "Tell your goddamned network that if they want to talk to me, raise their hands at a press conference. No more Mr. Inside stuff after that."
– Grade: F (too many words, doesn't apologize, and wouldn't have tried if it weren't for the damn mic)

You Get an Apology, You Get an Apology, You Get an Apology!

Then, of course, there are some folks who can't stop apologizing, since nobody accepts them. Such was the case with former senator Bob Packwood after accusations of making unwanted sexual advances while serving in Congress.

"If any of my ____________s *(noun)* or ____________s *(noun)* have indeed been ____________ *(adjective)* or if I have conducted myself in any way that has caused any individual ____________ *(disease)* or ________________ *(mental disorder)*, for that I am sincerely sorry. My intentions were never to __________ *(verb)*, nor to make anyone feel ________________ed *(emotional state)*, and I truly regret if that has occurred with anyone either on or off my staff."

When that didn't work, calls for his resignation continued. So on Dec. 10 '92 . . .

"This is clear. My past __________s *(noun)* were not only inappropriate. What I did was not just ____________ *(adjective)* or ________________ *(archaic adjective)*. My actions were just plain wrong. . . . Although most of these __________s *(noun)* are a decade or two decades old, and no one's __________ *(noun)* or __________ *(noun)* or __________ *(noun)* was __________ed *(verb)*, my conduct was wrong. I just didn't get it. I do now. The important point is that my __________s *(noun)* were ____________ *(adjective)* and ____________ *(adjective)*. These women (were) __________ed *(verb)*, appropriately so, and I am truly sorry. It was not done with ________________s *(cooking utensil)* or evil intent....If that requires professional __________ing *(verb)*, I will seek it. I guarantee that nothing like this will ever happen again."

Still no good, so he tried on Larry King's show, Mar. 30 '94 . . .

"What I was __________*ed* for—and again, I want you
verb)
to remember, Larry, at that time, the only charges were

the ____________ that ______________ had brought up. And of
(number 1) *(media source)*
the ____________, ______________ women, I didn't know. And none
(number 1) *(smaller number)*
of the __________*s* did I recognize as they talked about them. So what
(noun)
I __________*ed* for—and I'm paraphrasing it, because I can't remember
(verb)
[what] the exact words were—whatever it was I did, even if I couldn't remember it, I apologized for it. And I apologize again for it tonight. If I did things I can't remember, didn't know, or to people I didn't know, I'm ____________ and I apologize."
(adjective)

Packwood resigned a year and a half later, on Sep. 10 '95.

"Am I sorry? ____________. If I did the things they say I did, am
(affirmative)
I ____________? Do I __________? Yes. But it is time to get on and not look
(adjective) *(verb)*
back."

Are we done now? Good.

Hungry for Power: Al Gore Attempts to Steal the Election

Ever since the hanging chads of the 2000 election, we've had a new national pastime: accusing candidates of stealing elections. The next few pages contain highlights culled from various sources. Where to begin?

It is clear that the Democrats would not stop short of ______________ *(major crime)* to get Al Gore elected, so they can take __________s *(noun)* and ______________ *(negative verb)* our country. Just before the election, their __________s *(noun)* released a story involving a __________ *(crime)* conviction for George __________ *(letter)* Bush, but who among us has not __________ed *(verb)* while driving?

On Election Day itself illegal __________s *(group)* were allowed to vote, despite their inability to perform ______________ *(type of math)* in ______________ *(language)*. Then their ______________s *(term of affection)* in the media stepped in, calling Florida early in favor of Gore, thereby suppressing __________ *(group)* voters, who are known to become ______________ *(emotional state)* easily and don't like__________ing *(verb)* late in the day.

Did it stop there? No. They turned to a series of legal tricks involving ______________________ *(common household item)*, ______________________ *(chemical substance)*, and ______________ *(favorite food)*. They fabricated a "confusing ballot" controversy in ______________ *(fictional location)* County, arguing that simply because the ballots were written in ______________ *(dead language)*, voters over ______________ *(large number)* years old with weak ______________s *(body part)* might not recognize their __________ *(relative)*.

When Bush won the state by ______________ *(small number)* votes, they demanded a county-wide ______________ *(competition)*. ______________ *(group member)* lawyers even had the audacity to challenge absentee ballots from ______________ *(superhero team)*. They claimed Dick Cheney wasn't even a __________ *(species)*.

The Florida __________ *(group)* took the extraordinary step of bringing the case to ________________________ *(country and western singer)*. Democratic ________________s *(piece of clothing)* sought to exclude more than 200,000 legal and legitimate ballots from Florida's ______________ *(nonsense word)* and ______________ *(nonsense word)* counties, as well as Governor Jeb Bush's ______________ *(type of property)*. Thank goodness Katherine Harris evened things up by single-handedly ______________ing *(negative verb)* ______________ *(huge number)* votes that might otherwise have been counted.

In the end, George __________ *(letter)* ______________ *(type of plant)* was ahead in all of the polls by at least one percent, yet he lost the popular vote by ______________ *(huge number)*. Since he is president by __________'s *(deity)* will, and this is a __________________ *(type of government)*, how is that possible without cheating? Thank heavens ______________ *(powerful entity)* stepped in and put a halt to the ____________________ *(derogatory adjective)* recount. If only all ___________s *(evil act)* could be halted so easily.

Hungry for Power: Obama Attempts to Steal the Election

It is clear that the Democrats would not stop short of ______________ *(major crime)* to elect Obama, take power, and ______________ *(negative verb)* our country. As we speak, hordes of ______________s *(nut-gathering animal)* are descending on ______________ *(fast food place)* under the pretext of helping ___________s *(noun 1)* register to vote. No one is against ___________s *(noun 1)* voting, but ______________________? *(inhabitants of east coast state)* Didn't we just fight the ________ *(war)* against them and win?

John McCain's ____________ *(body part)* took aim, charging that the group should be ________________ed *(violent punishment)*. Campaign manager __________ *(Muppet)* also charged that a group called ________________ *(type of nut, all caps)* is engaged in widespread ______________ *(victimless crime)*.

Obama is not being honest about his ties to the group, which boasts registering some 1.3 million _______________s *(group member)*, often minorities and the poor, ignoring the fact that their own workers face charges of _______________ *(biological process)*. A host of other instances have been cited: fake names, dead people, even improperly registering _______________s *(stationary object)*.

Democrats say the charges are _______________ *(derogatory term)*. Many point to _______________ *(famous Republican)* insisting that he is rubber and they are glue. In ___________ *(theme park)* Attorney General _______________ *(cartoon character)* has filed a

lawsuit to try to force a ____________________ on the registration files.
(surgical procedure)

In a court filing this week, the state GOP said those checks should begin in __________. These cases recently indicate the workers faced a quota-type
(place)
system, receiving __________s for every ________________ of __________
(food) *(large number)* *(livestock)*
registered.

"For most of the individuals who have been hired to do this work, their primary focus is ________________," said ____________________, director
(body function) *(famous astronaut 1)*
of ________. "This was a ______________________ opportunity for them
(film) *(biological imperative)*
in tough economic times."

______________________ added, "If you have to come up with
(famous astronaut 1)
25 voter registration applications by the end of the day in order to ______________________, you're going to come up with the 25 voter
(biological imperative)
registrations."

Hungry for Power: Al Franken Steals Election

It is clear that the Democrats would not stop short of ________ *(major crime)* to elect Al Franken, take power, and ________ *(negative verb)* our country. After the initial count, Mr. Franken trailed Mr. Coleman by ________ *(short distance)* and ________ *(small number)* votes after the first ________ *(Olympic event)*.

The Democrats' strategy from the start was to ________ *(negative verb)* the recount in a way that would discover votes that could add to his ________ *(anxiety disorder)*. The Franken legal ________*s* *(insect)* swarmed the recount, aggressively demanding that votes that had been ________*ed* *(chemical process)* be added, while others were denied for Mr. Coleman.

The team's real ________ *(mineral)* mine was ________ *(complimentary adjective)* ballots, thousands of which the Franken team claimed had been ________*ed* *(verb)*. While Mr. Coleman's ________*s* *(relative)* demanded a(n) ________ *(occupation)* uniform, the Franken team ginned up an additional ________ *(container for liquid)* of absentees from the ________ *(household location)*. By the time this ________ *(cryptid)* hunt ended, Franken was ________ *(political office)* and Coleman left to ________ *(leisure activity)*.

What Franken understood was that ________ *(supernatural beings 1)* would be loath to overrule decisions made by ________ *(supernatural beings 2)*, however arbitrary those decisions were. He was right. The three-________ *(monster)* panel overseeing the Coleman ______________ *(type of fund)*, and the ______________ *(singing group)* who reviewed the panel's findings, found that Mr. Coleman hadn't demonstrated a willful or malicious attempt on behalf of officials to ______________ *(negative verb)* him and thereby deny him the election.

Mr. Coleman didn't lose the election. He lost his ______________ *(easy to lose object)*. ______________ *(science)* tells you that the recount totals always involve ______________ing *(creative process)*. In such a close election, the totals for both candidates should have been proportionately just as close if the process was ______________ *(complimentary adjective)*. However, Franken received over ______________ *(large number)* more votes, blowing proportion out of the water. Had Franken won by ______________ *(number)*, that would fall well within the realm of ______________ *(a fictional realm)*. But over 400? ______________ *(exclamation)*!

Clearly the fact that Franken won by more votes is an indication the election was ______________ed *(verb)*.

Ode to a Decider

Former president 43 was roundly praised for his contributions to the English language, actually receiving many awards. These "Bushisms" leave us in awe. We can't improve upon them, so here's a different challenge. Rather than hidden messages, can you unravel their intended meanings? Bonus points for complete sentences.

"I've been in the Bible every day since I've been the president."

"See, in my line of work you got to keep repeating things over and over and over again for the truth to sink in, to kind of catapult the propaganda."

"I didn't grow up in the ocean — as a matter of fact — near the ocean — I grew up in the desert. Therefore, it was a pleasant contrast to see the ocean. And I particularly like it when I'm fishing."

"Well, I think if you say you're going to do something and don't do it, that's trustworthiness."

"[Our enemies] never stop thinking about new ways to harm our country and our people, and neither do we."

"It's important for us to explain to our nation that life is important. It's not only life of babies, but it's life of children living in, you know, the dark dungeons of the Internet."

"I'm telling you there's an enemy that would like to attack America, Americans, again. There just is. That's the reality of the world. And I wish him all the very best."

"Too many OB/GYNs aren't able to practice their love with women all across the country."

"People say, 'How can I help on this war against terror? How can I fight evil?' You can do so by mentoring a child; by going into a shut-in's house and say I love you."

"I know the human being and fish can coexist peacefully."

"One of the great things about books is sometimes there are some fantastic pictures."

"I know how hard it is for you to put food on your family."

"I remember meeting a mother of a child who was abducted by the North Koreans right here in the Oval Office."

"Rarely is the question asked: Is our children learning?"

"We ought to make the pie higher."

"Fool me once, shame on—shame on you. Fool me—you can't get fooled again."

"I am surprised, frankly, at the amount of distrust that exists in this town. And I'm sorry it's the case, and I'll work hard to try to elevate it."

"I'm looking forward to a good night's sleep on the soil of a friend."

"So long as I'm the president, my measure of success is victory — and success."

"Thank you, Your Holiness. Awesome speech."

"I want to share with you an interesting program — for two reasons, one, it's interesting, and two, my wife thought of it — or has actually been involved with it; she didn't think of it. But she thought of it for this speech."

"First of all, I don't see America having problems."

"Oftentimes people ask me, 'Why is it that you're so focused on helping the hungry and diseased in strange parts of the world?' "

". . . when somebody makes a machine, it means there's jobs at the machine-making place."

"There's a huge trust. I see it all the time when people come up to me and say, 'I don't want you to let me down again.' "

"Anyone engaging in illegal financial transactions will be caught and persecuted."

"This thaw — took a while to thaw, it's going to take a while to unthaw."

"So I analyzed that and decided I didn't want to be the president during a depression greater than the Great Depression, or the beginning of a depression greater than the Great Depression."

"I'm going to put people in my place, so when the history of this administration is written at least there's an authoritarian voice saying exactly what happened."

"I'll be long gone before some smart person ever figures out what happened inside this Oval Office."

Misattribunals. The following have been attributed to Bush in error, but in fact come courtesy of the vice president to Bush the elder, Dan Quayle. Remember him?

The Holocaust was an obscene period in our nation's history. I mean in this century's history. But we all lived in this century. I didn't live in this century.

Republicans understand the importance of bondage between a mother and child.

Welcome to George W. Bush, Mrs. Bush, and my fellow astronauts.

One word sums up probably the responsibility of any governor, and that one word is "to be prepared."

I'm a Doctor, and I Play One on TV!

On March 17, 2005, our government was called into emergency session. Even President Bush returned from his vacation, setting the bar for interrupting his me-time. What was so important? A woman who'd been in a 15-year coma might die in the next couple of weeks. Luckily, the Senate had an expert witness on staff, majority leader and presidential candidate Bill Frist.

As most people know, this is coming to the floor very quickly. And the real, ____________ *(adjective)* reason is, if we do not act, a living ________________ *(plant or animal)* will be starved to death in a matter of days. That is why the action now. That is why we are, not rushing things, but ___________*ing* *(verb)* quickly, so we can get a bill to the __________________ *(shopping location)*.

She will be starved to death next Friday.

I have had the opportunity to look at the ___________________________ *(popular magazine or TV show 1)* upon which the initial facts of this case were based. And from my time as a(n) _____________ *(occupation)*, I would have to be very _________________ *(emotional state)* before I would come to the floor and say this, but the facts upon which this case were based are ____________ *(adjective)*. To be able to make a diagnosis of __________________ *(medical condition)* —which is not brain dead; it is not coma; it is a specific diagnosis, typically takes multiple examinations over a period of time because you are looking for _________________________ *(item from a scavenger hunt)* —I have looked at the _________________ *(type of media 1)*. Based on the _____________________________ *(popular magazine or TV show 1)* provided to me, which was part of the facts of the case, she does _________ *(verb)* if you poke her hard enough.

She has also not had a complete ____________________ exam
(medical specialty)

—allegedly, she has not had a ____________________ or ______________;
(exam procedure) *(type of test)*

not that those are definitive, but before you let somebody die, before you starve somebody to death, you want a complete exam and a good set of the facts of the case upon which to make that decision.

All we are saying today is, do not starve her ___________ to death
(adverb)

now, but establish the facts based on ___________________, and then
(crackpot theory)

make a _____________ in the future. That is what we will accomplish
(gift item)

by __________ing this __________.
(verb) *(noun)*

Note: the autopsy later found that, among other things, Terri's brain had shrunk to less than half the size of the average for her age — and about three-quarters of what Karen Ann Quinlan's was after 10 years in a similar state. It seems the video exam was not accurate.

Not to be outdone, running for her first term in Congress, Michele Bachmann explains her position, more than a year after the autopsy results were released.

I would've voted in favor of __________ing the ______________ of
(verb) *(body part)*

Terri Schiavo. She was a woman who was _____________, and she had
(adjective)

brain damage, there was brain damage, there was no question, but from a ________________________ point of view, she was not ___________ ill.
(comparative adjective) *(adverb)*

More Fun Than a Trunkful of Aliens

In November 2009 Lou Dobbs, long known for his xenophobic views, left his CNN show. Many hoped the tone of the conversation on immigration would become more measured. We all forgot about Arizona. Strange how what he said doesn't seem so bad now.

After complaints, Walgreens pulled "Illegal Alien" Halloween costumes from the shelves. Lou had a problem with that, since it is all about him.

"I'll tell you what's offensive, because it reminds people that there is such a thing as a(n) ________________ *(reviled group)*. And this is not to be ____________*ed* *(verb)* by the pro-amnesty, ______________ *(adjective)* amnesty groups. . . . They try to build this case that I'm some sort of __________ *(noun)*, even though they've never come up with a single ethnic slur, they've never come up with an instance of any __________________ *(abstract noun)* whatsoever in anything I've ever said and done."

OK, it isn't always about him. After CNN instructed that President Obama's birth was no longer a story, Lou went on the air with:

"______________ *(president)* promised ______________*s* *(noun)* and _______________ *(abstraction)* in his administration, yet he's chosen not to release his original _______________ *(type of art)* or even a copy of it. And a number of _______________ *(nationality)* are asking 'Why not?' The left-wing ____________________ *(reviled institution)* has attacked me because I asked the question."

Even when he wasn't raising questions, his statements were attracting attention.

"One of those ________________s out to advance the idea of
(reviled group)
liberal ________________ is none other than ________________. I
(political ideology) (reviled person)
thought we had gotten rid of this left-wing ______________ for a while,
(exotic animal)
but I guess he's ____________. I mean, he's a blood-sucking leftist. You
(adjective)
gotta put a _________ through his ____________ to stop this guy!
(noun) (body part)
So you've gotta give him credit for __________ing."
(verb)

When called out for using the phrase "blood-sucking liberal," he did the right thing and corrected: "I called him a blood-sucking leftist."

My Love Is Like a Red, Red Rose . . .

In July 2008 South Carolina governor Mark Sanford wasn't hiking the Appalachian Trail, as he said, but visiting Argentina with his lover. Hijinks ensued — divorce, resignation demands, yadda, yadda . . . Highlights included the love letters the governor was good enough to send on a state email account. That put them a Freedom of Information request away from publication, as *The State* discovered. How romantic can you make the governor?

____________,
(pet name)

Tomorrow leave at 5 am for ____________ (fictional location). Will think about you on its streets and wish I was going to be there later in the month when you are there.

I have been specializing in staying focused on decisions and actions of the ____________ (body part) for a long time now — and you have my ____________ (body part). You have oh so many __________s (noun) that pulls it in this direction. Do you really know how beautiful your __________ (noun) is? Have you been told lately how warm your __________s (body part) are and how they softly glow with the ____________ (adjective) nature of your soul? Above all else I love that ____________ (intangible quality) about you. As I mentioned in our last visit, while I did not need ____________ (emotion) fifteen years ago — as the battle scars of __________ (idiom) and __________ (noun) and __________ (noun) have worn on this has become a real need of mine. You have a particular ____________ (intangible quality) and __________ (noun) that I __________ (verb). You have a level of __________ (noun) that is so fitting with your __________ (noun). I could digress and say that you have the ability to give ____________ (adjective) gentle __________s (noun), or that I love your tan lines or that I love the curves of your ______________s (body part), the erotic beauty of you holding yourself (or two ______________ (adjective) parts of yourself) in the faded glow of night's light — but hey, that would be going into the sexual details we spoke of at ___________ (place) at dinner — and unlike you I would never do that!

I better stop now lest this really sound like the __________ (saga). Given I love you, I don't want to be part of the reason you are having less than an ideal week in what sounds like a cool spot.

In the meantime please __________ (verb) soundly knowing that despite the best efforts of my ______________ (body part) my ______________ (body part) cries out for you, your voice, your body, the touch of your body parts, the touch of your _______________s (body part) and an even deeper connection to your __________ (noun). I __________ (verb) you . . . sleep ______________ (adjective).

I Did Not Have Text with that Boy

In 2006 Congressman Mark Foley created a furor when it was discovered that he had inappropriate contact with a page. Foley promptly resigned, and after seeing his text messages you know why he did. Can you mentor as well as a congressman? Give it a try. Here is the *adult's* side of the conversation as provided to ABC News.

how my favorite young __________ doing
(noun)

did any girl give you a _____________ job this weekend
(body part)

did you _____________________ it this weekend yourself
(masturbation slang)

love details do you really do it face down

where do you ________________
(orgasm slang)

completely naked?

very nice

cute _____________ bouncing in the air
(body part)

i always use __________ and the hand but who knows
(noun)

just kinda slow _________*ing*
(verb)

well I have a totally stiff ________________ now
(erection slang)

but it must feel great ___________________ on the towel. is
(ejaculation slang)
your ___________________ limp . . . or growing
(slang body part)

so you got a ________________ now
(erection slang)

i am hard as a __________ *(geolith 1)* . . . so tell me when yours reaches __________ *(geolith 1)*

well tell me

ok . . . so what happens how does that ______________ *(porno slang)*

ha thats wild

what you wearing

um so a big ______________ *(erection sang)*

love to slip them off of you and grab the one ____________ *(body part)* __________ *(reptile)*

well your hard

and a little ______________ *(arousal slang)*

get a ruler and ________ *(verb)* it for me

thats a great size

still ______________ *(erection slang)*

take it out

ok

Can't Trust Those Presidents!

In September 2009, then Florida GOP chair Jim Greer ignited a media storm when he voiced his outrage that President Obama would dare address the students of America as they began the school year. Yeah, really! What nefarious plot would he hatch using our innocent children?

The idea that school children across our nation will be forced to watch the president justify his plans for ________________ *(offensive liberal plot 1)*, ____________ *(industry)* and ____________ *(junk food)* companies, increasing taxes on those who create jobs, and racking up more ____________*s* *(noun)* than any other president, is not only ____________ *(adjective)* but goes against beliefs of the majority of ______________*s* *(nationality)*, while ____________*ing* *(verb)* American parents through an invasive abuse of power. As the father of ____________ *(number)* children, I am absolutely appalled that taxpayer dollars are being used to spread President Obama's ________________ *(economic system)* ideology.

When asked how he knew the president's evil plans, he responded:

I think the speech he's gonna give Tuesday is gonna be significantly different than the one he was gonna give maybe ____________ *(number)* hours ago. The ____________*s* *(noun 1)* that he sent out . . . it does tie in, because that's what started everything. When the ____________*s* *(noun 1)* talk about writing how we can help President __________ *(noun)*, talk about his ________________ *(something to fear 1)*, talk about what he's done since he's become president and what makes you __________ *(verb)* him, and the initiatives he's put forth. That, to me, is an indication that his speech was going to talk about ______________________ (something innocuous 1). When you ask students to talk about how they can help him, versus how he can help them.

When the president and these ____________s (noun 1) talk about ____________________ (something to fear 1), ____________________ (something to fear 1) are what the vision of this, the president's, future is of this country. ____________________ (offensive liberal plot 1), __________ (noun) companies run by government, and before anyone exposes my children to their vision of America. But before any politician, Barack Obama included, talks to my children about ______________________ (something innocuous 1), I want to say yes, or no.

Where Are They Now

In June 2010 Greer was arrested for six felony charges including fraud.

In September 2010 President Obama gave much the same talk to students. No one said anything this time; they were busy screaming about other things by then.

Also largely unnoticed at this time, Jim Greer sent out a text message to the press saying, *"In the year since I issued a prepared statement regarding President Obama speaking to the Nation's school children, I have learned a great deal about the party I so deeply loved and served. Unfortunately, I found that many within the GOP have racist views and I apologize to the President for my opposition to his speech last year and my efforts to placate the extremists who dominate our Party today. My children and I look forward to the President's speech."*

Service! Service!

In 2010, Tea Party favorite Rand Paul won the Republican Party primary for governor of Kentucky. What he said about civil rights resonated with the right wing there but appalled much of the nation. To set the record straight, he went on *The Rachel Maddow Show*.

Maddow: If there was a ___________ *(business)* that wanted to not serve _________________s *(group member 1)* would you think they had a legal right to do so?

Paul: Yes. I would never belong to any club that excluded _________________s *(group member 1)*, but we still have clubs that discriminate based on _________________ *(human attribute)*. Should we limit speech from people we find abhorrent?

Maddow: But isn't being in favor of civil rights but against the Civil Rights Act a little like saying you're against high cholesterol but you're in favor of fried cheese?

Paul: I'm ___________ *(adverb)* in favor of the Civil Rights Act, but had I been around, I would have tried to ______________ *(negative verb)* it. Do you want to abridge the ___________th *(number)* Amendment? Can you have a(n) ______________ *(skin disease)* and say abhorrent things? The debate involves more than just _________________s *(group member 1)*. Many ________________ *(dangerous item 1)* organizations say they have a right to carry a _________________ *(dangerous item 1)* in a public restaurant.

Maddow: Let's say the owner of the swimming club says we're not going to allow ________________s. Unless it's illegal, there's nothing to stop that.
(group member 1)

Paul: Well, there's nothing right now to prevent a lot of __________ing.
(verb)
But does the owner own his ____________? Or does the government?
(body part)

Maddow: Should lunch counters have been allowed to stay segregated, yes or no?

Paul: To answer, you'd have to decide the rules for all ___________. But
(animals)
I think what you've done is bring up something that really is not an issue. It's a ________________ ploy. It's brought up as an attack weapon from
(college major)
the ____________s, and that's the way it will be used. But, you know, a
(monster)
lot of times these attacks fall back on themselves.

Maddow: Dr. Rand Paul, nominee for the ________________ in Kentucky,
(political title)
where he'll be representing not only his own ___________ on how to live
(group)
but what kind of ___________s we should have in America. Thank you.
(noun)

Heroine Worship

On January 13, 2010, Glenn Beck was over the moon to have former vice presidential candidate Sarah Palin on his show, causing him to wax poetic. Here are some snippets.

I want to read to you what I wrote last night in my journal, because it's about you. "Tomorrow I ____________ (verb) Sarah Palin and family for the first time. I'm actually a little ______________ (adjective), as she is one of the only ____________s (noun) that I can see that can __________ (verb) us out of where we are. I don't know yet if she's ______________ (adjective) enough, if she's well enough __________ed (verb), or if she knows she can no longer __________ (verb) anyone. I don't know if she can _____________ (verb 1) and not lose her ______________ (noun 1)." That is where I'd like to go for the next hour. Find out if this is the woman who can _____________ (verb 1) us and not lose her ______________ (noun 1).

That was just the intro. It gets creepier later on . . .

I wrote some notes here. You and I both were, I think, the number ____________ (number) and ____________ (number) ____________s (noun) of the year. Did you know that?

We both have been ____________ed (verb) on _______________________ (famous media source) for being ______________ (adjective).

We've also both been ______________ (adverb) voted onto the most ______________ (adjective) list of ____________s (noun) in the world.

We both have been on the cover of ___________s in the last year.
(noun)

We're both ____________________ top ____________
(emotional state) *(number)*
most ______________ ____________s in America.
(adjective) *(noun)*

We are both told that we "________________________," I mean
(judgmental phrase)
the list goes on, and on, and on.

Yes, a little clingy, but eventually there were some rambling questions.

. . . think of __________________, you don't trust it, think of
(landmark)
the __________________, I don't know if everybody
(social pillar)
___________s that anymore, think of the ______________________,
(verb) *(American auto)*
you don't _____________ that, think of the _____________
(verb) *(noun)*
you _____________. I have _____________ed in the last year
(verb) *(sense 1)*
particularly, I can't _____________ anybody, and I know the moment
(verb)
I _____________ed that, I can tell you the specific _____________,
(sense 1) *(place)*
and the specific _____________ . . . and I went __________________,
(noun) *(exclamation)*
I'm living in a(n) _______________ _____________.
(adjective) *(noun)*

Do you know that moment?

The Hannity Diaries: President Obama

No tour of the right would be complete without Sean Hannity. Here's an amalgam of quotes from his show reflecting his opinion of our current president.

I just want to say, while I believe it was a tremendous ____________ *(dance step)* forward and a great thing for the country to have elected an ____________ *(nationality)* -____________ *(religious follower)*, I still worry that the country does not know the "real" Barack Obama. And here's my other ____________ *(anxiety disorder)*-based fear. During the campaign, we saw a ____________ *(derogatory noun)* that followed a script from ____________ *(a movie)*. I think the real Barack Obama is, I fear, a ____________ *(nonhumanoid species)*, the guy that had these radical associations of 20 years, that knew ____________ *(dictator)*, ____________ *(serial killer)*, and ____________ *(cartoon character)*.

In order for Obama to win this election, he had to convince the ____________*s* *(group)* that the economy is in ____________ *(qualitative adjective)* shape and that's a lie. Bush left this country in ____________ *(make-believe place)*. We got out of the ____________ *(economic condition)* that Clinton gave us. Unemployment in this country was lower than it had been in the last four decades. Economic growth in Bush's last quarter was ____________% *(big number)*. Interest rates and inflation have been lower in the Bush years than in the last three ____________ *(units of time)*.

And today, the Obama administration rolled out the red carpet for a coalition of ________________ (type of criminal). Among the individuals in attendance was ______________ (evil person). That's the California man who sued unsuccessfully to have the words "under God" removed from ______________________________ (famous sex manual or dirty novel). Religious groups, however, have not received this kind of treatment from the Obama _________ (color) House. Just last year, the president distanced himself from the National Day of __________ing (verb 1), canceling the formal service traditionally held in honor of the day and refusing to attend a Catholic ________________ (leisure activity 1) breakfast. So what's going on? Has the administration demonstrated a pattern of ________________ (emotional state) toward religion, or is this merely a coincidence?

You put all of this in toto and we are looking at not only the socialization, the ________________ (foreign country)-ization of — the ______________ (hotel chain) socialist model coming to America, we're looking at the end of capitalism in America as ____________ (celebrity) knows it. I say this with all the sincerity and passion that I can muster up — he will go down in American history as the worst ______________ (occupation) we have ever had.

The Hannity Diaries: The Middle East

It's not just the president, as we see in this amalgam of Sean Hannity quotes, it's also certain segments of the world.

I have a hard time with the president's outreach to the ____________ *(group 1)* community. When he spoke to the ____________ *(group 1)* world, he didn't talk about America's contributions to ____________________ *(major corporation)*, he didn't talk about America's contributions to ____________________ *(type of investment)*, he didn't talk about America's contributions to ______________ *(politician)* or ____________________ *(cell phone brand)*. The fact is, I don't hear America being praised enough by the ____________ *(group 1)* world. Does the ____________ *(group 1)* world give America the ________________________ *(commodity or currency)* its due?

I think the Iraqis with all their ______________ *(commodity)* resources need to pay us back for their liberation. Every single solitary ________________ *(unit of currency)*. It should have been part of the deal. I think they owe us a lot for that.

Was the Iraq war ______________________ *(qualitative adjective)*? I believe when they took out ____________ *(number)* tons of yellow ________________ *(dessert food)* uranium from Iraq, that after ________________________ *(famous date in history)* it became a ________________ *(type of meal)* we couldn't take. We gave __________________ *(fictional villain)* a final opportunity to cooperate with ______________ *(rock singer)*, to allow the inspectors to do their ______________________ *(type of performance)*. He chose not to, so we responded with Operation __________________________ *(explosive onomatopoeia)* and ____________________ *(reverential noun)*.

And now there is a proposed ______________ near ground zero.
(retail outlet)
It's not just a bad idea, it's a(n) __________________ one.
(negative adjective)
Imam ________________ wants to "shred our Constitution" and replace
(cartoon villain)
it with ____________________. Allowing someone who thinks we made
(construction material)
up ___________________ and wants Sharia law preached at _________ is
(fictional character) *(place)*
a slap to the ____________ of ______________ families.
(body part) *(nationality)*

Obama has also pretty much given the go-ahead for Iran to pursue nuclear _________*s*. He says the ____________ world is full of people
(device) *(group 1)*
who want their ______________*s* to lead better lives. Of course it is.
(farm animal)
Some want their ______________*s* to grow up to be ______________*s*,
(farm animal) *(occupation)*
others want their children to grow up to be martyrs.

The Hannity Diaries: Global Warming

Domestic policy, foreign affairs, and science. Sean Hannity has it all as seen in this amalgam.

I believe America is the greatest country God ever gave ____________ *(famous Republican)*. I'm about what's right and wrong. I'm about looking at this ____________ *(derogatory noun)* for what it is. Global warming is the biggest scientific fraud, I think, in our ____________ *(household location)*. Sure, I want to end our dependence on foreign ____________ *(energy source)*, I want to drill in ____________ *(place)*, I want to go for nuclear ____________s *(appliance)*, I want to build ____________s *(toy)*, I want cars that run on ____________s *(minority group member)*. But we've learned a lot about the ____________s *(derogatory noun)* that lecture us about global warming, particularly Al Gore. If you look at Al Gore, he recommends we should ride our ____________s *(noun)* to work, yet he travels around the world in a ____________ *(science fiction device 1)*. You're going to lecture us about a car, and you're traveling in a private ____________ *(science fiction device 1)*?

And for our viewers up in the Arctic, it turns out there's no need to panic! All that ____________ *(something cold)* that's supposedly melted? It's been found! According to the National ____________ *(celebrity)* Fan Club it's been revealed that faulty ____________s *(group member)* caused them to underestimate the amount of ice by an area the size of ____________ *(celebrity)*'s ____________ *(body part)*. More global warming ____________ *(anxiety disorder)*. Ha!

Maybe it's just a coincidence that every global warming ______________ (happy event) takes place on the exact same day as a ________________ (natural disaster) or maybe ____________________ (Greek god or celebrity) is trying to tell these guys something. New information came out — this is the coldest ______________ (span of time) on record. Global warming, where are you? We want you back. Most people may buy in to Al Gore's movie, ________________ (science fiction film), but it's not reality and it's not __________ (science).

I'm Shocked, Shocked . . .

As we all know, Rush Limbaugh has always upheld the highest standards of journalism. That is why he was above reproach when he decides to instruct journalists in their craft, as seen in this collection of quotes.

"I mean, everyone in the world knows you don't believe anything on ____________ *(Web site 1)* because ________________ *(fictional character)* can go in there and put whatever ________________ *(dessert topping)* on that they want to, unless you succeed in getting your site locked, and I don't even care about that. ____________ *(Web site 1)* is as ____________ *(adjective)* as anything else. Anybody can post any __________*s* *(noun)* they want on there. But these are the ______________*s* *(occupation)*! They're supposed to check this stuff."

"Whatever happened to journalists calling people and saying, 'Did you __________ *(adverb)* say this?' They didn't want to take the chance I didn't say it. They wanted the excuse to run the fabricated _________ *(noun)*. These people are ____________________ *(derogatory adjective 1)*. They are literal professional ________________ *(derogatory noun)* and they are responsible in many ways for the ____________________ *(derogatory adjective 2)* standards and quality of journalism. They are...doing everything they can to promote _________ *(noun)* and _________ *(noun)* throughout our culture and society while holding themselves up as great _______________*s* *(occupation)* and people who care only about ________________ *(crackpot theory)*. When they're basically just ____________________ *(derogatory adjective 1)*, ____________________ *(derogatory adjective 2)*, impersonators of journalism."

But wait! Why then does Rush quote freely from the very encyclopedia he claims anyone can game? Fill in the blanks, yours will be just as accurate as the info Rush broadcast!

"Who is this judge? Judge ____________ *(person 1)* is a ____________ *(president)* appointee. Judge ____________ *(person 1)* is an avid ____________ *(profession 1)*. Do you know what a ____________ *(profession 1)* is? That's right. For our liberal caller today, this would not be good news. A ____________ *(profession 1)* stuffs dead game. If you go into a big, ____________ *(nostalgic location)*, you'll see some ____________ *(animal)* ____________ *(body part)* over the fireplace. A ____________ *(profession 1)* is responsible for it. After a 2002 ________*ing* *(verb)* trip during which he killed three ________*s* *(animal 1)* ____________ *(person 1)* had their ________*s* *(body part 1)* mounted over the door through which defendants must pass to enter the courtroom. At the time Judge ____________ *(person 1)* said the sight of the severed ____________ *(animal 1)* ________*s* *(body part 1)* would 'instill the fear of __________ *(deity)*' into the accused. The heads were removed in June 2003; it didn't even take a year [laughing] following complaints by local __________ *(noun)* rights groups."

Blankety Blanks: Sean Hannity

And now for another kind of blank! See if you can guess what Sean actually said in each quote below. Answer key at the bottom of the page.

"It doesn't say anywhere in the Constitution, this idea of ________."

"Governor, why wouldn't anyone want to say ________, unless they detested their own country or were ignorant of its greatness?"

"Soldiers are literally fighting for their lives and you don't have enough respect for them to take your protest somewhere else. . . . You have no respect for those guys that are trying to heal in that hospital. . . . Why don't you take your ________ and your ________ ________ and stop sticking it in the face of people that have suffered enough. Why don't you take it elsewhere?"

"Let me be straight with you — I like ________. I think he's a man of principle, a man of faith. I think he's got a backbone of steel and he's a real, genuine, big-time leader. . . . He's a consequential figure for his time. We don't see it right now."

"Clearly, we're out of the ________ that President Bush inherited."

"But the Alabama constitution, which Chief Justice Roy Moore is sworn to uphold, clearly it says, as a matter of fact, that the recognition of ______ is the foundation of that state's constitution."

"I'll tell you who should be tortured and killed at Guantánamo — ________."

"I never questioned anyone's ________."

Answers: the separation of church and state; the Pledge of Allegiance; protest; free speech rights; George W. Bush; recession; God; every filthy Democrat in the U.S. Congress; patriotism

Blankety Blanks: Ann Coulter

More direct quote blanks to horrify you! And who could be blanker than Ann Coulter? Answer key at the bottom of the page

"We should invade their countries, ________ their leaders, and convert them to Christianity."

"I think the government should be . . . engaging in ________ as a televised spectator sport."

"If only we could get ________ to boycott all airlines, we could dispense with airport security altogether."

"Bill Clinton was a very good ________."

"These people can't even wrap up ________. We've been hearing about this slaughter in Darfur forever — and they still haven't finished."

"God said, 'Earth is yours. Take it. ________ it. It's yours.'"

"Frankly, I'm not a big fan of the ________ Amendment."

"No, we just want ________ to be perfected, as they say. . . . That's what Christianity is. Jews."

"We need somebody to put rat poisoning in ________'s crème brûleé."

"It would be a much better country if ________ did not vote. That is simply a fact."

"Would that it were so! . . . That the American military were targeting ________."

Answers: kill; torture; Muslims; rapist; genocide; rape; First; Jews; Stevens; women; journalists

Why ________ Must Never ________

Sure, it's a free country, except for certain folks at certain times, who must at all costs be treated differently for their own good. Not a direct quote this time, but an all-purpose diatribe!

It's finally happened. President ________________ *(famous person)* pledged during his State of the Union address to "work with Congress and our __________s *(noun)* to change the law and allow __________s *(noun 1)* to __________ *(verb 1)*."

________________s *(left-wing group)* would have you believe that providing this right is simply a matter of ________________ *(abstract noun)*. But this is a historical prohibition that's lasted ________________ *(amount of time)* and is as much a part of our way of life as ________________ *(abstract noun)*. The Greeks had__________y *(noun)* the Romans had __________y *(noun 1)*, the English __________s *(noun)*. Even in the Bible, although __________y *(noun 1)* was widespread throughout the Roman world, Jesus never spoke out against it. Can we not say then that __________y *(noun 1)* is divine? That it brought Christianity to the __________ *(species)*, from across the ocean?

Since its foundation, our ______________ *(scary thing)*-fearing nation has stressed discipline, morale, order, and ______________ *(abstraction)*. Anything that adversely affects ____________ *(industry)* undermines that core. Moreover, a sudden change would have a profound and killing impact in a __________ *(service)* -based economy. The __________s *(plant)* would dry in the fields. ____________s *(product)* would cease being profitable. There will be widespread unemployment, chaos, uprisings, bloodshed, and ________________ *(something bad)*. Worse, the open presence of ________s (noun) in the close confines of a(n) ________ (small space) will undeniably create the possibility that ________ (type of energy) will be unleashed, undermining the very glue of our society, which the Greeks called ________ (word ending in -ology).

And what of the ________s (noun 1) themselves? They have their own honorable position, one accorded them by ________ (abstract force). Their proper sphere is ________ (location), where they might exercise their ________ (instinct). Wouldn't they be neglecting their ________ (noun) if they ________ed (verb 1)? Those who don't ________ (verb 1) are better cared for. Who would protect and assist them if they stopped? Is it better they be left to ________ (verb 1) helplessly for themselves?

Despite the arguments of ________ (derogatory adjective) scientists, many ________s (noun) believe that ________s (noun 1) are biologically incapable of ________ing (verb). And where does it end? If they're entitled to ________ (verb 1), should they also be allowed to ________ (verb)?

This is not my law, it is ________ (corporation)'s law, ________ (popular band)'s law, and ________ (reality TV show)'s law. In the end, ________ (group) will decide. I pray they do so in a(n) ________ (adjective) way. God bless you and God bless the ________s (noun).

Texas Larnacatin'

Larnin' is a little different in Texas (and bigger) where simple folk don't necessarily trust those science-type fellers. Could you pass the test from this imagined new textbook page?

Many theories attempt to explain the beginnings of life.

Some believe aliens visited the earth ________________ ago
(amount of time)
and mated with ___________s only to flee rather than pay for
(animal)
the ___________________s.
(thing a baby needs)

Some____________________ scientists believe the
(derogatory adjective)
amazing _______________ of life is completely ___________,
(abstract noun) *(adjective)*
that from a primordial _______________, exactly the right
(prepared meal)
combination of _______________s came together and formed the
(small thing)
first _________________ with no guidance whatsoever.
(electronic device)

Darwin's ____________________ book *Evolution of* _______________
(derogatory adjective) *(favorite food)*
puts forth the____________________ notion that mankind evolved
(derogatory adjective)
from __________________s in much the same way. If a certain type
(inanimate object)
of __________ with particularly large _____________s found it
(animal) *(body part)*
easier to _________, it would be more likely to reproduce, and its
(verb)
children would wind up with huge ______________s.
(body part)

Proponents of Intelligent Design, however, believe in the concept of "irreducible ___________y." (noun) They argue that life is not merely ______________________ (derogatory adjective) and is more akin to ______________________ (kindergarten activity). Like a machine, if one were to remove the __________ (noun) everything else in the system would _________ (verb). Therefore, there must have been some principle beyond ___________ (science) bringing it all together from the beginning, a principle with a longing for ______________________ (type of amusement).

Ultimately, since a __________ (noun) can hardly be called a fact, we are left to decide the truth for ourselves. But in the end, if there is no ________________ (famous actor) there is nothing to lose. Yet if there is, is it worth it to ignore Him, even on the slight chance you may spend all eternity in________________________________ (undesirable geographical location)?

I Was Against It Before I Was for It!

In January 2008, then CNN correspondent Glenn Beck entered the hospital for, in his words "surgery on my ass." It seemed to have left him a bad impression. According to the promos for his exposé, it was "a personal journey through the nightmare that is our health care system."

I'm ___________ing (*verb*) from some surgery that went horribly ___________ (*adverb*). I said on the way to the hospital, I said "if I die, ___________ (*superstitious phrase*), [and] this makes it into the paper I want to make sure this is not the way I'm remembered." And [it] almost happened. Not because of anything other than my desire to receive health care in the United States today. Even though I live in a very ___________ (*adjective*) area, this hospital . . . was ___________ (*adverb*) bad, the ___________s (*profession 1*) that treated me were ___________ (*adjective*). Many of the ___________s (*profession 1*) were ___________ (*adjective*). But I have some stories that will ___________ (*verb 1*) your ___________ (*body part 1*), and hopefully will ___________ (*verb 1*) the ___________ (*body part 1*) of the CEO of this hospital. I want this to be a cautionary ___________ (*noun*) to all of us, because this is one of the hospitals where the president of ___________ (*company 1*) goes. If they don't care about the president of ___________ (*company 1*), you really think they care about ___________s (*disney character*) that are just average working stiffs. It's ___________ (*negative adjective*).

Also, I probably had one of the ___________est (*adjective*) ___________s (*noun*) of my life, and I've had pretty ___________ (*negative adjective*) times. It's the only time in my life that I have had a ___________ (*biblical affliction*) that could have come out

of the movie __________. And it was jarring to me, to be a(n) __________
(movie) (adjective)
guy. It was so __________ to go from so much success, being convinced
(adjective)
that there is __________ no reason to live. That'll either screw you up
(adverb)
or it will open your ______________s. And I think it really opened
(body part 2)
my ______________s. I can't wait to share this with you. That and the
(body part 2)
coming ________________, and you know, stuff like that. We seem to be
(natural disaster)
a system now in health care that is just trying to ________ the ________
(verb) (noun)
out that door as fast as they can.

A few years later, when health care became an issue he could milk, he changed his tune.

June 4, 2008: "America already has the ______________est health care
(adjective)
in the world!"

April 29, 2009: "What does it mean for the rest of the world, if we loose our position as the __________, having the ______________est health care
(noun) (adjective)
in the world?"

May 12, 2010: "You're about to lose the ______________est health care
(adjective)
system in the world!"

Is Obama Really a ______?

Not born in the country, despite his birth certificate? Not a Christian, despite his church attendance? Now you can doubt whatever portion of President Obama's being you like! Can you be more inventive than the wing nuts?

A new poll suggests that one in five Americans still believes President Obama is a __________ *(noun)* despite the _______________ *(large object)* of evidence to the contrary. At the same time, the number of Americans who said they believed, correctly, that Obama is a __________ *(noun)* has declined from _________________ *(larger number)* percent to ________________ *(small number)* percent today. ____________ *(number)* percent of Americans now say they don't know what Obama's __________ *(noun)* is at all.

The Rev. Franklin Graham, son of __________________ *(movie monster)*, waded into the __________ *(noun)*, saying, "I think the president's problem is that he was born a __________ *(noun)*, his father was a __________ *(noun)*. The seed of _____________ *(fast food)* is passed through the father like the seed of ______________________ *(digestive medication)* is passed through the ____________ *(relative)*. He was born a _________ *(noun)*; his father gave him a(n) ____________ *(adjective)* name."

"Now it's obvious that the president has renounced the prophet ________________ *(famous golfer)*, has renounced _____________ *(bad habit)*, and accepted _________________________ *(Brady Bunch character)* as his personal ______________ *(occupation)*. I cannot say that he hasn't. So I just have to believe that the president is what he has said. However, the ______________________ *(Star Trek alien race)* world does sees the president as one of their ____________s_ *(occupation)*."

The president himself has written that his

father, ________________________ (superhero, Marvel or DC), was already a confirmed __________ (noun) by the time he was born. White House spokesman ________________ (movie director) reacted to Graham's comments, saying simply that the president is a committed __________ (noun) and that Franklin Graham is entitled to his ____________________ (type of door prize).

The misinformation continues to exist despite the president's own declarations of his deep faith in __________ (noun) and the statements of his ________________________ (supernatural creature) advisers. It is important to note that one in five Americans also cannot locate his or her own ______________ (body part) on a map, believes the earth is ____________________ (geometric shape), and that denial is a big river in Egypt.

Tear, Baby! Tear!

Randall Terry is the founder of Operation Rescue, a "leading pro-life Christian activist organization" dedicated to ending abortion. He's also notorious for using attention-seeking stunts to draw attention to his pet peeves. Lately, the topic is Islam. Specifically, Sharia law infiltrating the U.S. Oh, and he has jumped on the Tea Party bandwagon. He's now putting out training videos explaining how you, too, can desecrate a Koran for the betterment of America. Here's the narration from one.

Hello, friend, I'm ____________ *(person)*. In this __________________________ *(type of performance art)*, we are going to give you a demonstration of what we want you to do in your city. Now listen to me, there's a lot of people, millions of ______________ *(nationality)*, who are truly ______________ *(adjective)* about the direction that our country is in. They are ______________ *(adjective)* at what President __________________ *(famous person)* is doing. They are ______________ *(adjective)* at the way he _________s *(verb)* terrorists, the way he refuses to stand up to ______________________ *(extraterrestrial race)*. And, frankly, there's a lot of people ______________ *(adjective)* about his connection to the _________________ *(demographic)* world.

There are people who are ______________ *(adjective)* about Sharia law, about the ____________ *(religion)* terrorism that has plagued ____________ *(planet)* for decades now. There are people who _______________ *(active verb)* their _______________ *(body part)*, and they don't know what to do. Listen, you can have your voice heard. So we're gonna run through a little bit of role play. I'm going to show you exactly what we want you to do in your _________________ *(room in house)*.

To my fellow ______________________ *(political movement)* activists, listen to me: you're about to see instructions on how to get into real battles, not

just in front of our ___________s, not just ___________ing, but to
(noun) (verb)
go to the _________________ like ______________ and like other
(olde tyme place) 1700s person
great __________s did.
(noun)

In another video, he actually demonstrates how to tear and crumple paper.

So, you're talking to the _______________s, you say, I'm so and so,
(occupation)
then read them your signs with the passages from _______________,
(famous book)
and then, you say to the camera, "This is a(n) ____________ religion?
(adjective)
AAAHHhaaaaaa, haaahh haaaaaugh, aaahhhaah! That's hysterical,

haahhah! This is a peaceful religion?

Won't Somebody Think of the Children!

Ever vigilant, the right wing turned its focus on America's greatest enemy . . . babies! The only problem is nobody seemed sure how they were destroying America — by bringing aliens to our shores, or by growing up to become our enemy within.

On May 25, 2010, Arizona state senator Russell Pearce, always a font of new ideas on immigration, explained the issue to Bill O'Reilly.

The ____________________ *(Supreme Court case)* decision came before the ________________ *(gov't division)*, and it made it very clear to the ________________s *(elected official)* at the time, when the ____________th *(number)* Amendment was written, it did not pertain to ________________s *(type of doll 1)* and those who did not have legal domicile in __________ *(nation)*.

Other advocates of this proposition also took to the air to promote their cause. Attorney Wendy Murphy was on Fox News on July 28 to make the following case.

I know it's babies, and it's hard to be tough on babies, but let's remember we are talking about ________________ *(type of doll 1)* coming to __________ *(nation)* for the purpose of __________ing *(verb)* their child. Not that they _________ *(verb)* the kid, but 'cause they want to provide them with the benefits of U.S. ________________ *(abstract noun)*.

Birthright, I think, is a __________ *(noun)*. We should change our Constitution, and say if you come here ____________ *(adjective)*, and you have a ________________ *(type of doll 1)*, that ________________ *(type of doll 1)* is not automatically

a __________. They come here to drop a ____________________, it's
(noun) (familial relation)
called __________ and __________.
(verb) (verb)

When the idea failed to catch on, they upped the ante. After all, in these times, anyone can be a terrorist. Even a baby! On June 24, 2010, Rep. Louie Gohmert (R-TX) went to the floor of Congress to sound the alarm.

I talked to a retired _______________, who said what they're looking
(occupation)
at were ______________ cells in ______________ who have figured out
(adjective) (location 1)
how to __________ our system. And it appeared they would have young
(verb)
women, who became pregnant, would get them into ______________,
(location 1)
to have a __________________. They wouldn't even have to pay anything
(type of doll 1)
for the __________________. Then they will return, where they can be
(type of doll 1)
______________ and coddled as future ____________________. And then,
(adjective) (unpopular group)
twenty, thirty years down the road, they can be sent in to help __________
(verb)
our way of life.

Sorry, No Vacancy

With anchor babies posing such a credible threat to our nation, action is required. Lucky for us, we have the right people for the job.

Leading Republicans are considering revising the amendment granting citizenship to any ________________ *(Pokémon character)* born in the United States. Republican leader ________________ *(person in room)* of ________________ *(name of room you are in)* said he supports ________________*ing* *(negative verb)* the Fourteenth Amendment, although he emphasized that immigration focus should remain on ____________ *(fast food)* security.

"I'm not sure exactly what the ______________*s* *(occupation)* of the Fourteenth Amendment had in mind, but I doubt it was that somebody could ________________ *(mode of transportation 1)* in from ________________ *(imaginary place)*, have a __________ *(noun 1)*, and ________________ *(mode of transportation 1)* back home with that __________ *(noun 1)*, and that __________ *(noun 1)* is forever an American citizen," he said.

Repealing the right can be done only through constitutional ________________ *(biological process)*, requiring approval by two-thirds majorities in both chambers of Congress, three-fourths of the nation's ____________ *(livestock)*, and one-quarter of ________________ *(prominent corporation)*.

The proposals are sure to appeal to conservative ______________*s* *(occupation)* but could carry risks by alienating ______________*s* *(group member)* and alarming ______________*s* *(group member)* who could view constitutional

challenges as a(n) ____________________. __________ has become
(athletic competition) (group)
the largest minority in the United States, and many are highly driven

by ________________________.
(stimulating food or drug)

Defenders of the amendment say altering it would weaken

____________________ while doing little to deter
(famous bodybuilder)
________________________. Senate Democratic leader Harry Reid said
(super villain or monster)
Republicans were "taking leave of their ___________________."
(personal property)

_________________ recognized the risk, emphasizing that amending
(person in room)
the Constitution is a ____________ matter. "I believe that the Constitution
(adjective)
is a strong, complete, and ______________ crafted __________ that
(how adverb) (noun)
has ______________ governed our nation for centuries and any
(how adverb)
proposal to amend it should receive a __________________."
(sweepstakes prize)
They also suggested that as a compromise citizenship rights

be repealed only for _______________________.
(another person in room)

"We're not talking about simply abandoning them. In lieu of citizenship,

the children could be awarded ______________________, the ability
(a third world country)
to ______________, or simple a basket of _________."
(superpower) (food)

Guns in Starbucks: We Don't Need no Stinkin' Cappuccino!

After patrons began carrying weapons into Starbucks, despite a series of protests, the caffeine corporation stuck to its . . . uh . . . policy, but on March 3, 2010, it felt compelled to issue a statement, probably because the PR department was drinking too much coffee and couldn't sleep. The following bears only a slight resemblance to the original.

We at Starbucks recognize the significant and ____________ *(adjective)* passion surrounding the issue of open-carry ____________ *(weapon)* laws. Groups from both sides of this issue have chosen to use Starbucks as a way to draw attention to their ______________*s* *(sexual organ)* and away from our ethically sourced and highest-quality roasted arabica coffee.

While we deeply respect the ____________ *(currency)* of all our customers, Starbucks' long-standing commitment to _________ *(vice)* remains unchanged. We _________________ *(submissive verb)* with local laws in all the ______________*s* *(type of slum)* we serve. That means we abide by the laws that permit open carry of __________________*s* *(weapon or animal)* in ______________ *(large number)* U.S. states. Where these laws don't exist, carrying certain types of ___________*s* *(weapon)* in our stores is prohibited. However, patrons may still carry one hidden ___________ *(weapon)* for each _____________ *(coffee size)* beverage ordered.

While some may feel that ___________*s* *(weapon)* and the high amounts of ________________ *(stimulating drug)* in our delicious brews don't mix, may we suggest one of our new Kevlar __________________ *(article of clothing)*, offered at a discount in all participating stores.

At the same time, we have a security protocol for

any ______________ing event that might occur. Our staff of
(negative verb)
skilled ______________s are trained to call ______________ all
(occupation) (armed force)
by themselves, and at least one employee in each store is

well versed in ______________ perfectly capable of disarming
(martial art)
a(n) ______________ gunman with a swift flick of our delicious
(psychiatric condition)
espresso. Look for the barista dressed as a ______________
(macho Halloween costume)
and you know you'll be safe!

Were we to adopt a policy different from local laws, we would be forced

to ask law-abiding ______________s to leave our stores, putting them and
(noun)
our ______________ at risk. After all, who wants to face a
(type of goods or currency)
caffeine-stoked madman when he's carrying a ______________! In the
(weapon)
end, the political, policy, and legal debates around these issues belong

in the ______________, not in our comfortable, roomy, welcoming stores with
(place)
free Wi-Fi.

And remember, ______________s don't kill people, inferior coffee does!
(noun)

I Pledge Aliegummumble . . . mumble

Heading into the 2010 elections, the Republicans felt good about their prospects against the Democrats. However the Tea Party was threatening them from within. Convinced that if they could appeal to the Tea Party's visceral hatred for business as usual in politics, they'd be a lock, GOP leadership pledged to continue doing all the same things that annoyed the Tea Party in the first place. Check it for yourself at http://pledge.gop.gov.

America is more than ________________ *(abstract concept)*.

America is a(n) __________ *(noun 1)* — a(n) __________ *(noun 1)* that free people can ________ *(verb)* themselves, with a government whose powers are derived from the ________ *(noun)* of the governed and the conviction that each of us is endowed by their ________________ *(physical attribute)* with the unalienable rights to _________s *(noun)*, _________s *(noun)*, and the pursuit of __________________ *(attractive celebrity)*. America is the belief that any man or woman can — given ____________________ *(form of public subsidy)*, ________________ *(type of investment)*, and ________________ *(sandwich garnish)* — advance themselves, their families, and the common good.

America is a(n) ________________ *(type of land mass)* to those who ________ *(verb)* to be free and have the ________ *(asset)* and the ________ *(asset)* to determine their own destiny.

Whenever the agenda of government becomes ___________ *(adjective)*, it is the right of the people to institute a new ___________ *(auto part)* and set a different course.

These first principles were proclaimed in the ____________________ *(underground location)*, enshrined in the ____________ *(body part)* of ____________ *(comedian)*, and have endured through hard ____________ *(deli meat)* and ____________ *(dessert)* by generations of ________________s *(plant or animal)*.

In a self-____________ing *(verb 1)* society, the only __________ *(noun)* against the power of __________s *(noun)* is the consent of the ____________ing *(verb 1)*, and regarding the policies of the current government, the ____________ing *(verb 1)* do not consent.

A(n) ____________ *(adjective)* and out-of-touch government of self-appointed ______________s *(occupation)* makes decisions, issues ______________ *(medication)*, and enacts laws without ____________ing *(verb)* or ____________ing *(verb)* the __________ *(noun)* of the many.

A rising __________ *(noun)*, crushing __________ *(noun)*, and a(n) ____________ *(adjective)* political environment are ____________ing *(verb)* the bonds among our people and ____________ing *(verb)* our sense of national purpose.

We pledge to __________ *(verb)* ourselves to the task of reconnecting our ____________ *(adjective)* __________ *(noun)* to the permanent truths of ______________ *(fantasy author)* by keeping faith with the __________ *(noun)* our nation was ____________ed *(verb)* on, the ____________s *(noun)* we stand for, and the ____________s *(noun)* of our people. This is our pledge to ___________ *(nation)*.

This Is No Time for New Ideas!

The 2010 Montana Republican Party platform is quite an ambitious document. Can you help them tell us what we are doing wrong?

MONTANA REPUBLICAN PARTY PLATFORM | Adopted June 2010

AGRICULTURE

We ________ those actions that would ________ the safety and
(verb) *(verb)*
protection of Montana's agriculture from ________*s*, ________*s*,
(noun) *(noun)*
and ________*s*. We strongly oppose the ________ ________ or
noun) *(adjective)* *(noun)*
augmentation of any threatened or endangered species.

AMERICAN INDIAN AFFAIRS

We support the creation of a Republican ________ task force to meet
(ethnicity 1)
with ________*s* and develop party positions pertaining
(member of ethnicity 1)
to ________ issues. We support Republican values education
(ethnicity 1)
in ________ country. We recommend that the Republican
(demographic 1)
National Committee establish an ________ caucus and fund
(ethnicity)
Republican values education in ________ country.
(demographic 1)

BUSINESS AND LABOR

We believe that prosperity results from ________,
(patriotic noun)
and that unencumbered ________*ism* is the
(noun)
most ________ method of allocating ________*s* and setting
(adjective) *(noun)*
fair ________*s* and ________*s* with a minimum of government
(noun) *(noun)*
interference and ________ .
(hated activity)

We believe in ________ in government.
(Chinese food)

HOMOSEXUAL ACTS

We support the ____________ right of the people of ____________________
(adjective) (imaginary location)
expressed by _____________ to keep homosexual acts illegal.
(superhero)

MEDICAL USE OF MARIJUANA

We recognize that a(n) ____________ problem exists with
(adjective)
____________________'s current laws regarding the ______________
(imaginary location) (adjective 1)
use of marijuana and we _________ action by the _____________
(verb) (gov't body)
to _________ or repeal the ______________ Marijuana Act.
(verb) (adjective 1)

EDUCATION

Curriculum that emphasizes the American _________________ system.
(patriotic noun)

The teaching of ___________ and __________ history, along with
(nation) (state)
__________________ of our state and nation, should be taught at all
(patriotic fixation)
levels.

HEALTH CARE

We support the repeal of the __________________s, commonly known
(torture device)
as ____________ -care.
(dictator)

IMMIGRATION

We support the strict interpretation of the _____________th Amendment
(number)
and the denial of ____________ to those here illegally.
(garnish)

Why the Republicans Will Win in 2012

In late 2010, continued unemployment and low poll numbers for the Democrats gave Republicans even more hope of scooching themselves into the driver's seat of our national bus. What follows is a typical expression of those good feelings.

Remember ________ (*war*)? ________________ (*national tragedy*)? Oh yeah, good times will be back! Time was when the ________________ (*type of mass media*) had everyone convinced Bush botched things, but the thin ________s (*noun*) of those lies are fading fast! The Democrats have taken things too far ________ (*direction*), ensuring the right will return!

The ________________ (*human organ*) stimulus bill, __________ (*prefix*)-spending, death ________s (*furniture*), and the lies being told about health care reform will choke off the far left. Senior ________s (*animal*) should be the most worried because they are ________________ (*derogatory adjective*). Your ____________ (*body parts*) will be gone by the time you finish reading this sentence!

Meanwhile in their ________________ (*evil organization*) meetings Democrats use ________s (*monster*) to keep citizens from speaking while Obama acts like ________ (*actor*), telling people to ________________ (*negative verb*) themselves if they do not like his ________ (*noun*), even threatening to destroy them with his ________________ (*object of vast power*). And people don't even know if he's a ________________ (*group member*) or even born on __________ (*planet*)!

The Democrats are not here to protect the ____________________
(endangered species)
of the U.S. They are here just to make laws that appease themselves and

their ________________________________. They do not care if they ruin
(pagan god or entertainment figure)
this great country, which is ___________ in health care, ___________
(ranking) (ranking)
in high school graduates, and ___________ in personal freedoms, according
(ranking)
to a recent poll by my ___________!
(relative)

Each time the ________________s battle, they grow stronger.
(group member)
Their cyber, grass, and _________-roots grow _________________________er.
(prefix) (complimentary adjective)
Each time Obama, Reid, and ____________ defy _________________ and
(rock star) (religious figure)
use their ______________s to ram through unpopular legislation,
(magic item)
frustration and anger rise.

Sensible people with old time ______________s need to take over.
(body part)
People like _______________, _________________, and __________________,
(WWII leader) (Greek general) (fictional leader)
who will repeal the ____________th amendment, restore our right
(number)
to drill in ______________s for oil, illegalize ____________________,
(body part) (basic human right)
and immediately invade __________________.
(foreign nation)

It's coming people and I for one can't wait!

The End of the World as We Know It: Michele Bachman on Overdrive

Michele Bachman, U.S. Representative from Minnesota's Sixth District, has been a stunning source of bizarre statements. What follows is not an actual speech, but a "best of" collection based on actual quotes. Whatever you come up with is sure to pale with the original words, which appear following.

First let me say that not all ___________s (*noun*) are created equal. I look at ___________ (*book or TV show 1*) and I give it more credence than my own ___________ (*body part*). It just seems to me we're seeing the fulfillment of the Book of ___________ (*comedian*) here in our own time, where every man is doing that which is right in his own ___________ (*place*) — in other words, anarchy.

Isn't it ___________ (*negative adjective*) when a(n) ___________ (*occupation*) can say to ___________ (*size*) children that you can't say ___________ (*children's song*) but must learn that ___________ (*a street drug*) is normal and should try it? All schools will soon begin teaching homosexuality. But the fact is, if you're involved in the gay and lesbian ___________ (*noun*), it's ___________ (*adjective*) bondage, ___________ (*adjective*) despair, and ___________ (*adjective*) enslavement.

It is equally horrific to know that among the ___________ (*group*), 50 percent of all ___________ (*relatives*) in the United States end in abortion, 50 percent.

As for plagues, I also find it interesting that in the 1970s ___________ (*contagious disease*) broke out under another Democratic president, Jimmy Carter. I'm not blaming this new epidemic on President Obama, I'm just saying it's ___________ing (*adjective*).

Meanwhile, death panels are the bureaucracies that President Obama is establishing where ______________s (occupation) will make the decision on who gets __________ (drug) and how much. How can they be trusted to do the right thing, when, for example, a ______________ (vegetable), Terri Schiavo, was healthy. There was ______________ (body part) damage, there was no question. But from a health point of view, she was not terminally ill.

______________________________ (obvious environmental hazard) is also wrongly portrayed as harmful. But there isn't even one study that can be produced that shows that ________________ (fatal disease) is harmful.

What is the solution? For starters, I wish the ______________________s (supernatural being) would take a great look at the views of the people in Congress and find out: Are they pro-____________ (sport 1) or anti-____________ (sport 1)?

Also, if we took away the minimum wage—if conceivably it was gone—we could potentially virtually wipe out ___________ (group) completely because we would be able to offer ____________s (noun) at whatever level.

Likewise, __________________________ (member of age group 1) should be paying his employer because of broken ____________s (noun) or whatever _________ (sin) occurs during that period of time. But you know what? After six months, that __________________________ (member of age group 1) is going to be a ______________________ (comparative adjective) employee and is going to go on a trajectory where he's going to be making so much _______________ (vegetable 1), we'll be borrowing _______________ (vegetable 1) from him.

As for the energy tax, I want people armed and _____________________ (negative adjective).

We need to fight back. Thomas Jefferson told us "having __________ every
(drug)
now and then is a good thing," and the people — we the people

— are going to have to fight back hard if we're not going to lose

our ______________s.
(frozen food)

As I say, I just take ____________________ for what it is. I recognize
(book or TV show 1)
that I am not a(n) ______________. I'm not a(n) ________________________
(occupation) (complimentary adjective)
thinker on all of this. I wish I was. I wish I was more knowledgeable, but

I'm not. Thank you and __________ __________ ____________.
(deity) (verb) (nation)

We had a hard time doing justice to Rep. Bachman, as seen on the previous pages. So, just this once, here are the original texts straight from the horse's mouth. Did your responses do her justice?

First let me say that not all cultures are created equal. I look at the Scripture and I give it more credence than my own mind. It just seems to me we're seeing the fulfillment of the Book of Judges here in our own time, where every man is doing that which is right in his own eyes—in other words, anarchy.

Isn't it bizarre when a judge can say to little children that you can't say the pledge of allegiance but must learn that homosexuality is normal and should try it? All schools will soon begin teaching homosexuality. But the fact is, if you're involved in the gay and lesbian lifestyle, it's personal bondage, personal despair, and personal enslavement.

It is equally horrific to know that in the African American community, 50 percent of all African American pregnancies in the United States end in abortion, 50 percent.

As for plagues, I also find it interesting that in the 1970s swine flu broke out under another Democratic president, Jimmy Carter. I'm not blaming this new epidemic on President Obama, I'm just saying it's interesting.

Meanwhile, death panels are the bureaucracies that President Obama is establishing where bureaucrats will make the decision on who gets health care and how much. How can they be trusted to do the right thing, when, for example, a woman, Terri Schiavo, was healthy. There was brain damage, there was no question. But from a health point of view, she was not terminally ill.

Meanwhile, carbon dioxide is wrongly portrayed as harmful. But there isn't even one study that can be produced that shows that carbon dioxide is a harmful gas.

What is the solution? For starters, I wish the American media would take a great look at the views of the people in Congress and find out: Are they pro-America or anti-America?

Also, if we took away the minimum wage — if conceivably it was gone — we could potentially virtually wipe out unemployment completely because we would be able to offer jobs at whatever level.

Likewise, teenagers should be paying the employer because of broken dishes or whatever occurs during that period of time. But you know what? After six months, that teenager is going to be a fabulous employee and is going to go on a trajectory where he's going to be making so much money, we'll be borrowing money from him.

As for the energy tax, I want people armed and dangerous. We need to fight back. Thomas Jefferson told us "having a revolution every now and then is a good thing," and the people — we the people — are going to have to fight back hard if we're not going to lose our country.

As I say, I just take the Bible for what it is. I recognize that I am not a scientist. I'm not a deep thinker on all of this. I wish I was. I wish I was more knowledgeable, but I'm not.

Thank you and God bless America.

South Carolina Candidate Andre Bauer on Food Stamps

In January 2010, a certain Republican gubernatorial candidate had some interesting things to say about the social safety net, at one point comparing the poor to animals. Here's an article recapping the moment in all its social Darwinist glory.

Lt. Gov. Andre Bauer, running for governor of South __________ *(place)*, had some __________ *(bathroom adjective)* things to say about the food stamp program, questioning whether it should be free. "Why shouldn't you have to __________ *(verb)* to get them?" Bauer asked of people receiving food stamps, free school lunches and public __________ *(type of performance)*. "In government, we are too often giving a __________ *(body part 1)* out instead of a __________ *(body part 1)* up."

Bauer said giving __________ *(candy 1)* to needy _________s *(noun)* means encouraging dependence. It also gives the recipients a license to have children who will also be dependent on public aid, he said. "My __________ *(relative or pet)* was not highly educated, but she told me as a __________ *(size)* child to quit feeding stray _________s *(group member)*," Bauer told a Greenville-area crowd. "You know why? Because they breed. They breed like __________ *(porn star)*."

"You're facilitating the problem if you give an animal or a person an ample __________ *(candy 1)* supply. They will __________ *(biological function)* and __________ *(biological function)* all over the place, especially ones that don't think too much further than that. And so what you've got to do is you've got to ________ (verb) that type of behavior. ________s (animal) don't know any better. Soon there will be ________s (group member) in ________ (place), ________ (political party members) in ________ (place), and ________ (religious followers) in ________ (place). And I mean all over the damn ________ (place). You know what I'm saying? And who will clean up the mess?"

When various groups condemned Bauer's choice of ________s (relative), he retracted his statements, saying, "Okay, maybe not ________s (animal). And maybe my phrasing was awkward, but the real question is, Is Andre Bauer ________ (sexual preference)? That is now the story," he said. "We're a long way from where we were a week ago."

Oh, What Is It This Time?

In the summer of 2010, heading into a midterm election, a previously ignored construction project involving an Islamic center being built near the former site of the World Trade Center became front-page news. To some it was a sacred site, to others a place to watch strippers. Certain newspapers were only too happy to stir up unrest with items like the one below.

Yesterday, ________________ *(abstract noun)* was ___________*ed* *(verb)* and __________*s* *(verb)* by a group of __________ *(noun)* Americans determined to erect a ___________ *(number)* -story ________________ *(place of evil 1)* a stone's throw from the spot where nearly 3,000 innocents were slaughtered in the name of religion.

It's nothing to cheer.

________________ *(place of evil 1)* advocates claim that this exercise in religious will and real estate ________________ *(abstract noun)* was an example of a people __________*ing* *(verb)* their __________________*s* *(consumer item 1)*. It was not.

Yesterday's 9–0 vote by the ______________________ *(fictional organization)* to deny the site landmark status essentially __________*ed* *(verb)* the site and delivered it into the hands of the ______________ *(evildoers 1)*. This was the latest __________ *(noun)* against those who _________ *(verb)* at the thought of seeing a(n) ______________ *(evil place 1)* rise atop their loved one's _____________ *(body part)*.

For months, ______________ *(evil place 1)* opponents have watched ___________ *(adverb)* as _______________ *(evildoers 1)* do everything but stick _____________________ *(bondage equipment)* in their ______________*s* *(body part)*. Where I come from, that's called __________*ing* *(verb)*

one's right to protest. The right to ________________? If you object
(consumer item 1)
to the mega-________________, you have none.
(evil place 1)

When the vote was over, a(n) ______________ found the courage to
(occupation)
shout to ____________________s, "Did any of you _________ anyone
(cartoon character) (verb)
on _________?" It was too late.
(date)

Critics, including ________________ of the ____________________,
(famous person) (famous organization)
have been demonized as "___________s." And not just by ___________s.
(noun) (monster)
Mayor ___________, the _______________'s chief booster, suggested that
(person) (evil place 1)
those who oppose it are dumb __________s.
(noun)

Neighbors have a right to know what the devil is moving in next door.
Still a mystery is where the __________________ will get
(derogatory noun)
the $________________ in construction costs needed.
(large number)
Imam ___________________ told ______________ reporters the funds
(cartoon character) (nationality)
will be homegrown — but told the foreign press that money will be
raised from ______________________. On radio, he refused to say he
(alternate dimension)
believed _______________________ to be a terrorist group.
(children's organization)

I thought people had a right to _________ authority. That right has
(verb)
been ____________ed by the Ground Zero ______________.
(verb) (evil place 1)

Dick Morris on the Ground Zero Mosque

Gorillas travel in a gang, dolphins in a pod. What do Republican pundits travel in? Limousines, generally. Here's one having his say on the Ground Zero Mosque controversy.

The proposed ______________ *(house of worship or retail outlet)* near ______ *(place)* would be — as many ______________ *(fast food restaurants)* are — a terrorist recruitment, indoctrination, and training center. It is not the worship of ______________ *(god or type of currency)* that is the problem. It is the efforts to ________ *(verb 1)* Sharia. There is a global effort to ________ *(verb 1)* Sharia and make it the legal system of ________ *(place)*. In the United Kingdom, for instance, many courts recognize Sharia as the governing law on matters between two ______________s *(animal or children's toy)*.

Most major ____________s *(retail outlet)* and financial institutions offer Sharia-themed ________ *(food)*. Imam ______________ *(cartoon character)*, the founder of the proposed mosque, helps prepare a Sharia index that rates ______________ *(good or service)* on their degree of compliance with Sharia law.

Not only is Sharia a vicious anti-female code that orders death by ________ing *(verb)*, promotes ________ *(noun)* marriage, decriminalizes abuse of women, and gives wives no ________ *(weapons)* in divorce, but it also explicitly recognizes the duty of all ______________s *(group member)* to wage jihad against nonbelievers and promote ______________ *(a popular product)* to achieve its goals. Jihad is as inherent in Sharia as ______________ *(architectural style)* is in ______________ *(form of government)* doctrine.

But there are non-Sharia mosques where ______________ (complimentary adjective) and ______________ (complimentary adjective) Muslims worship in their own way without promoting horrors such as ______________ (a spectator sport). Twenty percent of the mosques in the United States have no taint of Sharia and simply promote peaceful ______________ (method of dying).

There can be no doubt that any mosque organized and run by Imam ______________ (cartoon character) will be based on __________ (novel) and will serve as a local branch office of the ______________ (brand name) terrorist offensive against the West. That such a facility should be located right next to __________ (place) where jihad achieved its most hideous triumph is ______________ (negative adverb) ______________ (negative adjective).

______________ (political title) Obama is confusing the ______________ (demographic) when he describes the issue as one of ______________ (fashion style) freedom. There is broad latitude to worship God as ______________ (Republican) chooses, but none to promote violence and terrorism.

Dr. Laura Has Left the Building

On August 10, 2010, Anita Hanson, an African American married to a white man, gave Laura Schlessinger's radio show a call asking for advice. What she got led to Schessinger's decision, days later, to retire from radio to, in the doctor's words, "regain my First Amendment rights."

CALLER: I'm having an issue with my husband. I'm __________ *(color)* and he's __________________ *(different color)*. Some of his friends and family make racist __________________________________s *(sound emanating from human body 1)*.

SCHLESSINGER: Well, can you give me an example of a racist ____________________________________ *(sound emanating from human body 1)*?

CALLER: Last night we had a(n) ______________ *(occupation)* come over, and it's always a comment like, "Oh, well, how do you _________________s *(derogatory noun 1)* like doing this?"

SCHLESSINGER: I don't think that's racist. A lot of ____________________s *(derogatory noun 1)* voted for Obama simply 'cause he was half-____________________ *(derogatory noun 1)*. Didn't matter what he was gonna do in office, it was a(n) ____________________ *(derogatory noun 1)* thing. You gotta know that.

CALLER: How about the N-word? So the N-word's been thrown around —

SCHLESSINGER: Black guys use it all the time. Read ___________________ *(major newspaper)*, turn on _________________ *(news network)*, listen to a __________ *(color)* comic, and all you hear is _________________ *(expletive 1 3X)*. We've got a ____________ *(monster)* as president, and we have more complaining about racism than ever. I mean, I think that's hilarious.

CALLER: So it's okay to say _____________ *(expletive 1)*? Is it ever okay to say that word?

SCHLESSINGER: ______________s talking to each other seem to *(derogatory noun 1)* think it's okay.

CALLER: But you're not a(n) ______________ *(derogatory noun)*. My husband is.

SCHLESSINGER: Oh, I see. So ______________ *(expletive 1 3X)* is restricted to race.

CALLER: I can't believe someone like you is on the radio spewing out ______________ *(expletive 1)*.

SCHLESSINGER: I didn't spew out the ______________ *(expletive 1)* word.

CALLER: You said ______________ *(expletive1 3X)*.

SCHLESSINGER: Right, I said that's what you hear. ______________ *(expletive 1 3X)*

CALLER: Everybody heard it.

SCHLESSINGER: Yes, they did. They did, and I'll say it again — ______________ *(expletive 3X)*.

CALLER: So what makes it —

SCHLESSINGER: Why don't you let me finish a ______________ *(part of grammar)*? You know what? If you're that hypersensitive and don't have a sense of humor, don't marry a ______________ *(derogatory noun 1)*. If you're going to marry out of your race, people are going to say, "Okay, what do ______________s *(derogatory noun 1)* think? What do ______________s *(color)* think? What do ______________s *(animal)* think?" And what I just heard from the caller is a lot of what I hear from ______________ *(derogatory term 1)*-think — and it's really distressing and disturbing. I didn't call anybody a ______________ *(expletive 1)*. Nice try. Actually, sucky try. ______________ *(expletive 1 6X)*.

God's Final Warning in 2008

For our last official fill-in, an oldie but a goody. Much as the wing nuts dabble in conspiracy, the pros have been predicting the end of the world for thousands of years. They do it so often, and with such vehemence, we sometimes wish the world would end, just so we wouldn't have to hear from them anymore. Here's one of the latest, or one of the oldest, depending on how you look at it.

__________ *(year)* marked the last of ______________ *(pagan god)*'s warnings to __________ *(species)* and the beginning in a countdown of the final ________________ *(amount of time)* of man's self-rule that will end by ______________ *(holiday sale)* 2012.

On ________________ *(your birthday)* 2008, the first ____________________ *(musical instrument)* of the seventh ___________ *(animal)* of the ________________ *(type of media)* of revelation sounded, which announced the beginning collapse of the _____________ *(appliances)* of the United States and the great __________ *(movie)* that will follow.

The next three ________________s *(type of media)* will result in the ____________ *(adjective)* collapse of the United __________s *(noun)*. Once the fifth sounds the world will be thrust into ___________ *(TV show)*. The seven ____________________ *(musical instruments)* of the seventh _______________ *(sea mammal)*, as well as the seven ______________s *(type of beer)* of the book of _________________ *(famous author)*, which the apostle __________________ *(famous comedian)* saw but did not actually read, will be revealed in the last episode of *Larry King Live*.

Many of the prophecies of ______________________ *(amusement park ride)* are being ___________s *(verb 1)* and will continue to __________ *(verb 1)* throughout this season on __________________ *(all-news network)*. The prophecies revealed

explain the demise of ________________, ______________,
(famous animal) (theme park)
and all _______________s_, which will be followed by
(cute animal)
______________________'s final _________.
(name of person in room) (meal)

This last _______________ will be the result of _________ing_
(coveted object) (verb)
religions and the ______________ they sway.
(retail outlets)
Billions will _________________! The _________ of this time will
(undesireable verb) (noun)
far exceed the very worst seen in the history of ________________.
(popular sitcom)
As these events unfold, the _________ will increasingly become
(group)
aware of the authenticity of ____________________ and realize
(failed political figure)
that ______________________________ had been sent by God
(Republican currently seeking office)
as His end-time prophet.

Blankety Blanks: Rush Limbaugh

Not shocked by the real world yet? Here are some more direct quotes, this time from Rush, proving once again that truth is stranger than parody. Answer key below.

"Take that ________ out of your nose and call me back."

"Look, let me put it to you this way: the NFL all too often looks like a game between the ________ without any weapons."

"More people have died at ________ than have died at nuclear plants."

"I want him to fail, if his agenda is a far-left collectivism, some people say ________, as a conservative heartfelt, deeply, why would I want ______ to succeed?"

"Feminism was established to allow ________ easier access to the mainstream."

"The difference between ________ and yogurt is that yogurt comes with less fruit."

"Have you ever noticed how all composite pictures of wanted criminals resemble ________?"

"Obama's got a health care logo that's right out of ________ 's playbook."

"The only way to reduce the number of ________ is to use them."

Answers: bone; Bloods and the Crips; Chappaquiddick; socialism; unattractive women; Los Angeles; Jesse Jackson; Adolf Hitler; nuclear weapons

Suggested Word List

Activity
Counseling
Hunting
Philately
Speed Walking

Act of Congress
Civil Rights Act
Clean Water Act
Dingley Act
Menominee Restoration Act
Patriot Act

Addictive Drug or Food
Chocolate
Cocaine
Coffee

Adjective
Bushy
Existential
Fruity
Fundamental
Lacy
Polarizing
Xenophobic

Affiliations
Christian
Democrat
Free mason
NFC Partisan
Patco Member
Republican
Teabagger
Zoroastrian

American Icon
Bald Eagle
Fanny Pack
Hot Dog
Stars & Bars

Animal
Aardvark
Tapir
Annoying Animal
Chihuahua
Lindsay Lohan
Cute Animal
Bush Baby
Lemur
Endangered Species
Polar Bear
Tiger
Famous Animal
Flipper
Lassie
Taco Bell Chihuahua
Farm Animals
Chicken
Llama
Sheep
Fast-Breeding Animal
Rabbit
White Trash
Livestock
Cow
Pig
Republicans
Reptile
Lizard
Snake
Donald Trump
Sea Mammal
Manatee
Otter
Snookie
Whale

Archaic Adjective
Boorish
Hottentot
Rakish

Archetype
Fool
Hero
Sage
Trickster

Architectural Style
Bauhaus
Federalist
Neo-Classical
Neo-Manueline

Bad Habit
Spitting
Talking in Movie Theater
Voting on Reality TV Shows

Basic Need
Air
Cable TV
Food
Unlimited Minutes
Water

Beverage
Chocolate Phosphate
Coffee
Kombucha
Soda

Biological Function
Elimination
Farting
Locomotion
Respiration
Biological Imperative
Eating
Reproduction
Television

Bodily Fluid
Adrenaline
Bile
Ichor
Phlegm

Body Part
Cloaca
Eye
Head
Heart
Naughty Bits
Appendages
Antennae
Arms
Fingers
Internal Organ
Pancreas
Stomach
Thalmus
That Squiggily One
Sexual Organ
Pistil
Stamen
(what did you expect, eh?)

Bondage Equipment
Ball Gag
Comfy Chair
Handcuffs
Licorice Whip
Rope

Book
Moby Dick
Mules and Men
The Rat
Ulysses

Novel
Elmer Gantry
The Hobbit
I Served the King of England
Saga
Beowulf
Dune
The Godfather
One Hundred Years of Solitude
The Thornbirds

Burdens
Child Care
Health Insurance
Income Taxes
Oil Dependency
Parents
Property Taxes
Sales Tax
Thinking

Capital Equipment
Copier
Forklift
Truck
Appliance
Microwave
Mr. Coffee
Refrigerator

Cartoon Character
Bugs Bunny
Felix the Cat
Fritz the Cat
George Jetson
Homer Simpson
Jimmy Neutron
Snoopy
SpongeBob SquarePants

Chemical Substance
Acetylsalicylic Acid
Calcium Carbonate
Iron Oxide
Sodium Stearoyl Lactylate

Civil Right
Right to Fair Trial
Right to Party
Right to Property
Right to Work

Civil Service Group
Air Traffic Controllers
Postal Workers

College Major
Drinking
Hotel Management
Philosophy
Sports Management

Comedian
Lewis Black
George Carlin
Larry the Cable Guy
Chris Rock
Lily Tomlin

Commodity
Bauxite
Gummi Bears
Sugar
Pork Bellies

Common Household Item
Chair
Cup
Magic 8-Ball
Monkey Butler
Toothbrush

Competition
The Amazing Race
Pike's Peak Hill Climb
Presidential Election

Contagious Disease
Consumption
Line Dancing
Meningitis
Plague

Country Singer
Brooks & Dunn
Toby Keith
Taylor Swift

Coveted Object
Monkey Butler
Neighbor's Ass
Neighbor's Maanservant

Crackpot Theories
Creationism
The Da Vinci Code
Evolution
Flat Earth
Free Speech
The Illuminati Conspiracy
Scientific Method
Supply-Side Economics
The Zombie Apocalypse

Crime
Major
Fraud
Murder
Rape
Minor/Petty
Loitering
Open Container
Victimless
Stealing from the Blind
Wearing White After Labor Day

Currency
Drachma
Goats
Pound
Rubles
Yen

Dangerous Item
Circular Saw
Hand Grenade
Wolverine

Deity
Anubis
Ganesh
God *(you know, the real one)*
Hercules
Jupiter
Shiva

Demographic
African Americans
Asians
Media Elites
Them
Yankees Fans
Zoroastrians

Digestive Medication
Pepcid
Pepto-Bismol
Tabasco
Tums

Easy to Lose Object
Car Keys
Dreams
Elephant
Small Child
Umbrella
Virginity
Wallet
Your Mind

Economic System
Capitalism
Free Enterprise
Underground
Virtual

Elected Official
Dog Catcher
Governor
Grand Poobah
Library Trustee

Electoral Methods
Gibbard–Satterthwaite Theorem
Preferential Voting
Rock, Paper, Scissors
Weighted Voting

Electronic Device
The Clapper
Computer
GPS
Television

Emotional state
Ennui
Happy
Hate
Love

Energy Source
Coal
Hamster Wheel
Hydroelectric
Oil
Wind

Ethnicity
African American
Aryan
Atlantean
Hobbit
Latino

Euphemism
Crossing Over
Diffrently Abled
Minimally Exceptional
Operational Exhaustion
Sleep with the Fishes
Take You for a Ride

Evil Act
Kicking Midgets
Voting Democratic
Voting Repubican
Watching Fox News

Evil Organization
European Union
Fox News
Freemasons
Justin Bieber Fan Club
United Nations

Exam Procedure
Blood Test
Colonoscopy
MRI Scan
Phrenology
Pull My Finger

Food
Apple Pie
Escargot
Fried Butter
General Tso's Chicken
Pancake and Sausage on a Stick
Shawarma
Tandoori Chicken

Form of Government
Democracy
Junta
Kleptocracy
Theocracy

Geolith
Rock
Sediment
Stone

Geopolitical Division
Alaska
Bolivia
East Germany
Maginot Line
Persia

Government Agency
Court of International Trade
Dept. of Motor Vehicles
Dept. Public Works
Endowment for the Arts
FBI
State Department

Government Institution
Congress
Earmarks
Post Office
Supreme Court

Group
Cubs Fans
Family
Friends
Furries
Politicians
Shriners

Hackneyed Phrase
Give 110%
Go for It
No "I" in team

Hated Activity
Colonoscopy
Homework
Regulation
Thinking

Hated Group
Democrats
Pedophiles
Scientists
Teabaggers

Holiday
Boxing Day
Diwali
Purim
Thanksgiving
Weasel Stomping Day

Holy Book
The Bible
Dianetics
Dungeon Master's Guide
Mahabharata
Qur'an

House of Worship
Church
Mosque
Scientology Celebrity Center
Stupa
Temple

Hyperbole
Destroying Our Country
Hates Our Freedoms
Wants Us to Fail

Idiom
Against the Clock
Down the Drain
Game Over
Kick the Bucket

Illegal Profession
Bookie
Drug Dealer
Hit Man
Mouseketeer

Illness
Consumption
Dropsy
Epstein-Barr Virus
Munchausen by Proxy
The Vapors

Imaginary Country
Liliput
Mordor
Shangri-La
USA...USA...USA...

Infinitive
Happen
Possibly
Reveal

Institution
Church
Wal-Mart

Intangible Quality
Inner Beauty
Je Ne Sais Quoi
Truthiness
Well-Being
Wisdom

Landmark
Angkor Wat
The Capitol Building
Corner Store
Courthouse
Gas Station
Mount Rushmore
Reagan Birthplace
Stonehenge

Language
Cantonese
English
Esperanto
Klingonese
Latin

Leadership Title
Capo Di Tutti Capi
Coach
Lord High Chancellor
Oh Captain, My Captain
Prime Minister

Legal Procedure
Attachment
Billing
Enforcement
Overbilling
Service

Local Organization
AAA
BBB
Boy Scouts
Oddfellows
Shriners

Location
Downtown
Over There
Upstairs

Magic Item
The Constitution
The One Ring
Temple Garments
Wand

Media Source
American Idol
Cat Fancy
Modern Bride
The New York Times
NPR
Saturday Night Live
USA Today

Medical Specialty
Anterior-Segment Cornea Surgery
Dentistry
Dermatology
Neurology
Phrenology

Movie
Breakin' 2: Electric Boogaloo
Death Race 2000
Eat Pray Love
Jaws
Pricilla, Queen of the Desert
The Shawshank Redemption
White Heat
Science Fiction
Alien
Forbidden Planet
The Matrix
Star Wars

Muppet
Beaker
Cookie Monster
Kermit
Statler

Musical Group
The Beatles
The Harmonicats
The White Stripes
Wu-Tang Clan

Musical Instrument
Didgeridoo
Oboe
Slide Whistle
Vuvuzela

Nationality
Congolese
Earthican
Navajo
Romulan
Tuvaluan

National Tragedy
9/11
Civil War
Hurricane Katrina
Sarah Palin
Super Train

Natural Force
God
Gravity
Nature
Time

Nonsense Word
Gobbledegook
Hummannahummanna
Oojie-Boojie

Nostalgic Location
Abu Ghraib Prison
All-Male Club
Behind the Henhouse
Colored's Waiting Room
Friars' Club
Mom's House

Nouns
Asians
The Bible
Bigamy
Broccoli
Chickens
Children

Double-Wide
English
Illegal Immigrants
Ivory
Muslims
Slavery
Walk-in Freezer
Women

Abstract Nouns

America
Belief
Freedom
Hatred
Justice
Liberty
Philosophy
Salvation

Object of Great Power

Atomic Bomb
Burrito
Excalibur
Large Hadron Collider
Mom
The One Ring

Obvious Environmental Hazard

Loose Plutonium
Mountaintop Removal
PVCs in Groundwater

Occupation

Astronaut
Carny
Corporate Yes Man
Horse Whisperer
Lawyer
Oral Surgeon
Paranormal Investigator
Tree Surgeon

Offensive Liberal Plot

Charity
Medicare
Social Security

Olde Tyme Place

Haberdashery
Milliner's
Slave Quarters
The Stocks
Town Square

Olympic Event

Floor Exercise
Luge
Syncronized Swimming

Outdated Concept

Hoop Skirts
Monarchy
Pants on Monkeys

Patriot Fixation

Christian Nation
Constitution
Flag
Founders
Founding Fathers

Pejorative

Airhead
Schmuck
Worthless

Person

Author

Günter Grass
Stephen King
Snookie

Celebrity

Justin Bieber
Paris Hilton
Michael Moore

Dictator

Nicolae Ceaușescu
Kim Jong Il
Stalin
Your Favorite Democrat
Your Favorite Republican

Fictional Character

Barney Fife
Carrie Bradshaw
Darth Vader
Elmo

Fictional Leader

Burger King
George W. Bush
David Palmer
Emperor Palpatine

Mobster

Vito Corleone
Fat Tony
John Gotti
Dutch Schultz

Personal Luxury

Bathysphere
Ferrari
Motor Yacht

Pet Name

Pookie
Snookums
Whazzername

Place

Attic
Beauty Salon
Cyber Shop
Latrine
Oval Office
Pyramids at Giza
Rain Forest
Sesame Street
Stonehenge

Political Ideology

Anarchy
Communism
Democracy
Socialism

Political Title

Il Duce
The Honorable

Psychological Disorder

Bulimia Nervosa
Dissociative Disorder
Munchausen by Proxy
Schizophrenia

Really Boring Sport or Activity

Curling
Football
Hunting

Religion

Cheondoism
Christianity
Druidism
Jediism
Scientology
Zoroastrianism

Religious Figure

The Fonz
L. Ron Hubbard
Your Favorite Pope
Your Favorite Republican

Retailer

Amazon
Harrods
Macy's
Target

Reviled Group

Democrats
Illegal Aliens
The Media
Scientists

Reviled Person
- Adolf Hitler
- President Carter
- President Clinton
- President Obama
  - Oh, Any Democrat...

Science
- Chemistry
- Biology
- Physics
- Scientology

Science Fiction Device
- Compassionate Conservative
- Corbomite Device
- Privatization
- Time Machine
- Transporter

Sex Manual or Smutty Novel
- Fear of Flying
- Kama Sutra
- Story of O
- What the Parrot Saw

Sexual Activity
- Bestiality
- Bondage
- Dress-up
- Intercourse
- Oral Sex
- Watching

Sexual Preference
- Bisexual
- Furries
- Hetrosexual
- Homosexual
- Xenosexual

Sin/Deadly Sin
- Envy
- Gluttony
- Greed
- Lust
- Pride
- Sloth
- Wrath

Social Pillar
- Facebook
- Courthouses
- Churches
- McDonald's

Sport
- Basketball
- Badminton
- Jai alai
- Soccer

Sport Equipment
- Ball
- Quaffle
- Shuttlecock
- Wicket
- Xistera

Sport Position
- Beater
- Goalie
- Midfielder
- Point Guard

Sports Term
- Curly Shuffle
- Full Court Press
- Hail Mary

Surgical Procedure
- Appendectomy
- Liposuction
- Vasectomy

Title for a Dictator
- Bababooey
- Generalissimo
- Hero of the Fatherland
- President

Type of Investment
- 401k
- Bonds
- Collateralized Debt Obligation
- Pyramid Scheme

Unlikely Occurrence
- Graduate
- Inquire
- Learn
- Listen
- Rapture
- Think

Unpopular Group
- Democrats
- Fanfic Writers
- Pedophiles
- Republicans

Verbs
- Baste
- Carom
- Chase
- Drive
- Gain Citizenship
- Gerrymander
- Juggle
- Lead
- Live
- Meet
- Regurgitate
- Serve in the Military
- Speak
- Vote
- Whittle

Vice
- Cocaine Addiction
- Jersey Shore
- Killing for Pleasure
- Pederasty
- Polygamy
- Smoking

War
- Boer War
- Crimean War
- Franco-Prussian War
- World War I
- The Big One
- The War for Middle Earth
- Mole Creatures vs. Surface Dwellers

Weapon
- Boomerang
- Harpoon
- ICBM
- Slingshot